Disposed to Learn

ALSO AVAILABLE FROM BLOOMSBURY

Multiculturalism and Education, Richard Race
Analysing Underachievement in Schools, Emma Smith
Ethnicity, Race and Education: An Introduction, Sue Walters

Disposed to Learn

Schooling, ethnicity and
the scholarly habitus

**MEGAN WATKINS AND
GREG NOBLE**

B L O O M S B U R Y
LONDON · NEW DELHI · NEW YORK · SYDNEY

Bloomsbury Academic

An imprint of Bloomsbury Publishing Plc

50 Bedford Square
London
WC1B 3DP
UK

175 Fifth Avenue
New York
NY 10010
USA

www.bloomsbury.com

First published 2013

© Megan Watkins and Greg Noble, 2013

British Library Cataloguing-in-Publication Data
A catalogue record for this book is available from the British Library.

ISBN: HB: 978-1-4411-6245-8
PB: 978-1-4411-7711-7
ePub: 978-1-4411-3006-8
ePDF: 978-1-4411-7020-0

Library of Congress Cataloging-in-Publication Data
Watkins, Megan.
Disposed to learn : schooling, ethnicity and the scholarly habitus /
Megan Watkins and Greg Noble.
pages cm
Includes bibliographical references and index.
ISBN 978-1-4411-7711-7 (pbk.) – ISBN 978-1-4411-6245-8 (hardcover) –
ISBN 978-1-4411-3006-8 (epub) – ISBN 978-1-4411-7020-0 (pdf)
1. Educational anthropology. 2. Educational sociology. 3. Multicultural education.
I. Noble, Greg. II. Title.
LB45.W296 2013
306.43'2–dc23
2013006862

Typeset by Newgen Imaging Systems Pvt Ltd, Chennai, India
Printed and bound in Great Britain

Contents

Acknowledgements

This book was only possible through the involvement of a large number of people. First we would like to thank all the school staff, parents, students and community representatives involved in the study upon which this book was based. In particular we would like to thank the teachers who allowed us into their classrooms to observe their practice and were happy to assist us in obtaining the data we required. Thanks also to the staff in each of the homework centres we visited.

The research informing this book was drawn from an Australian Research Council (ARC) Linkage Project with the Multicultural Programs Unit (MPU) within the New South Wales (NSW) Department of Education and Training (DET). We worked closely with a number of staff at the MPU during the course of this project: Hanya Stefaniuk, Amanda Bourke and Nell Lynes who provided invaluable support, guidance and advice. They were terrific partners to work with, and their input was critical at all stages of the research. We would also like to acknowledge other NSW DET personnel – Greg Maguire, Seini Afeaki, Soo Humphries and Mary Binder – who each contributed at early stages of the project. Thanks also to Lucy Hopkins, Inga Brasche, Cristyn Davies, Neil Hopkins, Pat Bazeley, Parlo Singh and Mike Horsley who provided assistance in the initial framing, collection and analysis of the data. Much needed administrative support was also provided by Mary Corkhill and Maree O'Neill. Our research has been greatly assisted by working in the wonderfully productive research environment of the Institute for Culture and Society (formerly the Centre for Cultural Research) at UWS with numerous seminars and workshops informing the ideas that have framed this book.

We also want to acknowledge each of the following and to thank the publishers for permission to reproduce sections from each of these within this publication:

Watkins, M. and Noble, G. (2011), The productivity of stillness: composure and the scholarly habitus. In D. Bissell and G. Fuller (eds), *Stillness in a Mobile World*. London: Routledge, 107–24; Watkins, M. and Noble, G. (2011), Losing touch: pedagogies of incorporation and the ability to write, *Social Semiotics*, 21(4), 503–16; Watkins, M. (2011), Complexity reduction, regularities and rules: grappling with cultural diversity in schooling. *Continuum: Journal of Media and Cultural Studies*, 25(6), 841–56; Watkins, M. (2010), Discipline, diversity and agency: pedagogic practice and dispositions to learning. In Z. Millei, T. G. Griffiths, and R. J. Parkes (eds), *Re-Theorising Discipline in Education: Problems, Politics and Possibilities*. New York: Peter Lang, 59–75; Noble, G. and Watkins, M. (2009), On the arts of stillness: towards a pedagogy of composure. *M/C Journal*, 12(1); Cardona, B., Watkins, M. and Noble, G. (2009), *Parents, Diversity and Cultures of Home and School*. Centre for Cultural Research, University of Western Sydney; Watkins, M. and Noble, G. (2008), *Cultural Practices and Learning: Diversity, Discipline and Dispositions of Schooling*. Centre for Cultural Research, University of Western Sydney.

Alison Baker and Rosie Pattinson at Bloomsbury have also been great to work with and we are extremely appreciative of their support and patience particularly during the final stages of preparing the manuscript for publication.

Finally, we would like to acknowledge the financial support of the ARC, the NSW DET and the University of Western Sydney. The public funding of research is essential to the ongoing task of redressing educational inequalities and achieving educational excellence in schools. We hope this book has made some contribution towards developing a greater understanding of key issues in meeting these goals.

ACKNOWLEDGMENTS

Introduction

There is a common perception that students from specific cultural and linguistic backgrounds – what is conventionally referred to as 'ethnicity' – have a predisposition towards educational achievement. Students from 'Asian' backgrounds, for example, are often seen as having a cultural advantage, while others, such as Pasifika students, are perceived as culturally prone to underachievement.[1] There are assumptions about 'Asian values' of education, family and hard work (Robinson, 2000; Yu, 2006; Kim, 2010; McClure et al., 2011) and beliefs about how 'Asian' students have greater 'natural' abilities, particularly in maths and science, which are recycled in the media on a regular basis. These claims treat ethnicity as referring to fixed and bounded 'groups', and see educational achievement as a result of the inherent psychological and even biological qualities of these 'groups'. Drawing on research into students of Chinese, Pasifika and Anglo backgrounds in Australia, this book challenges these claims, and examines the relations between ethnicity and dispositions towards learning from a quite different perspective. In contrast to common assumptions about the pre-given attributes of some ethnic groups, it considers how home and school practices help produce the attributes of learners, how these attributes are embodied as dispositions towards learning and how the successful acquisition of these dispositions – what we call the scholarly habitus – is patterned in terms of ethnicity and broader sociocultural background.

The Australian experience has direct relevance for other, especially Western, migrant nations. Australia has one of the largest per capita migrant populations in the world, and it is also one of the most culturally diverse, with 27 per cent of the population born overseas from over 200 countries (Australian Bureau of Statistics (ABS), 2011). Against the trend, Australia has also maintained its commitment to multicultural policies, placing a strong emphasis on multicultural education (Australian Government, 2011). Both in Australia and elsewhere, however, the relationship between ethnicity and education is a complex one that, we suggest, has not been fully explored, and research into the links between ethnicity and educational outcomes has been uneven (Strand, 2007; Windle, 2008). Claims have long been made about the educational *dis*advantage attached to migrant and ethnic background (de Lemos, 1975). It quickly became clear, however, that the evidence was much more complicated, indicating differences between students with a language background other than English (LBOTE) were often more significant than those between them and English-speaking background (ESB) students (Martin and Meade, 1979). In the 1980s, some researchers began claiming that there was a distinct *advantage* experienced by LBOTE students (Birrell, 1987).

An analysis of the data, however, shows that there is no universal factor of ethnicity related to achievement but a complex relationship between ethnicity, language, socio-economic status (SES), gender, generation, family contexts and histories of migration. Our purpose is not to review this extensive literature: this has been done many times (Kalantzis and Cope, 1988; Windle, 2004; Strand, 2007) but rather to caution against the reductive use of ethnicity in explaining educational performance and to suggest that broad correlations can only be a starting point for analysis. Use of notions of 'ethnicity', 'culture' and 'race' in aggregating educational statistics often turn complex socio-historical processes and relations into 'things' that, as a result, seem to be coherent and seem to have explanatory value. Simplistic claims have long been made about the educational consequences of ethnicity, positive and negative. Bullivant (1987, 1988), for example, has argued that the 'ethnic success ethic' or 'migrant drive' is the determining factor in the success of those with a LBOTE, claiming that the personal motives for leaving one's homeland translates into specific aspirations and hence an educational advantage for young LBOTE people. This may be the case in some instances, but it doesn't explain poor outcomes for other groups, such as Pasifika students in Australia, New Zealand and the United States, and Black Caribbean and Muslim students in the United Kingdom and Canada. Moreover, reductive links between 'ethnic motivation' and educational success mean that the complex aspects noted above are obscured (Windle, 2004, p. 276).

Similarly, the notion of discrete 'learning styles' has reinforced a common idea that there are culturally specific attributes that shape educational outcomes (Jensen, 1988; NSW Department of School Education, 1992; Mangina and Mowlds, 2007; Charlesworth, 2008). This literature often makes broad claims about the psychological and neurological bases of these attributes in ways that essentialize and pathologize ethnicity and culture (Gutierrez and Rogoff, 2003). As Sue and Okazaki (1990) demonstrate, the success of 'Asian' students has often been explained, inadequately, in terms of hereditary differences in intelligence, or in terms of enduring cultural values. Despite the extensive critiques of these approaches (Poynting and

Noble, 1998; Coffield et al., 2004) they retain both academic and popular purchase. Apart from both the questionable assumptions about the cognitive and pedagogical values of notions of 'learning styles', they repeat the problematic assumption of the coherence of a nation-based 'culture' and its continuity with diasporic communities after the experience of migration and generational change.

Despite these qualifications, there are connections between ethnicity and educational achievement for some groups. The educational success of Chinese migrants to Western nations (Costigan et al., 2010; Pang et al., 2011) and the poor educational outcomes of Pasifika students (Flockton and Crooks, 2001, 2003; Horsley and Walker, 2004) are demonstrated through research. Often raised in debates about these outcomes is the part played by shared cultural values (Sue and Okazaki, 1990). Yet Rosenthal and Feldman (1991) critique claims that a simple notion of cultural difference can be used to explain the contrasts in educational performance between 'Chinese' and 'Western' students in Australia and the United States, given the scope of these categories, and that the importance of family environment is due to a combination of factors. Similar findings are evident in the United Kingdom (Francis and Archer, 2005).

These links need to be addressed but in more complex ways than popular myths, statistical correlations and learning styles research would suggest. Wu and Singh (2004), for example, explore the phenomenon of 'wishing for dragon children' associated with Chinese parents. They argue that this desire for the educational success of their children derives not simply from Confucianism, as is often claimed (Grimshaw, 2007) but relates to the historical role of the civil service and its educational system in dynastic China, and to the reinvention of this system under the Communist regime in the 1970s. Moreover, they suggest that the reproduction of this desire among the Chinese-Australian diaspora often reflects the dynamics of migration for white-collar workers who are unable to have their qualifications recognized, and so shift their energy to their children's educational success, fostering, for example, the growth of coaching colleges and the intensification of competition for selective high school places. Sue and Okazaki (1990) similarly argue that blocked mobility for Chinese migrants is crucial to the increasing value given to the educational success of their children. The creation of family environments in which there are strong demands for educational achievement, values of effort, restraint and industry (Rosenthal and Feldman, 1991), then, is less to do with overarching, ethnically defined values than a complex of factors and the link between family attributes and the institutional practices of the educational system (Louie, 2004).

The lives of Pasifika groups in Australia, while also shaped by processes of migration and settlement, tell a different story, involving social and economic disadvantage, educational underachievement and criminality far removed from their homeland experiences (Francis, 1995; White et al., 1999; Dooley et al., 2000; Singh and Sinclair, 2001). Media coverage has been given to the increasing incidence of crime and the relationship between this and low levels of school retention (Hildebrand, 2003; Hall, 2009), and 'Asian' students are sometimes compared with Pasifika students in terms of educational success, here and overseas (AAP, 2002; Fisher, 2011; Pang et al., 2011). Yet, as Coxon's (2007) account of education in Samoa demonstrates, educational structures and practices cannot be explained by some primordial and unified system of cultural values, but by complex and changing histories. In Samoa, a 'traditional' focus on the teacher as an authority who must be respected and not challenged, deriving from the hierarchical structure of village life, is being challenged by the recent shift to a child-centred focus and 'active' pedagogies introduced as part of a modernizing process that itself relates to a history of colonization, decolonization and economic underdevelopment. Any claim that the 'cultural values' of migrants from places like Samoa entail communal values of cooperation and sharing, needs to address more closely the specificity and contingency of educational and cultural practices. Yet it is not just that the problematic attribution of certain values to specific cultures needs to be questioned, but a larger issue about the way we conceptualize notions of culture and ethnicity and their explanatory value.

From cultures to cultural practices

Part of the problem in thinking through the links between cultural background and educational experience is the terminology used. 'Ethnicity', 'culture' and 'race' are all complex and problematic terms evoked in discussions about educational (and economic and social) disadvantage. Each is often assumed to be an unproblematic category based on clear boundaries around particular groups of people and their values and customs.

As has been well documented over several decades, 'race', as delineating a genetically homogenous group of people, while historically dominating modern Western conceptions of colonized peoples, has become increasingly untenable both as a scientific category and as a term of political rhetoric (Goldberg, 1993). In Australia, it is a category that is declining in use, especially in relation to migrant populations: it may feature in accounts of Indigenous and non-Indigenous relations but increasingly these too are discussed in terms of cultural difference (Hollinsworth, 2006). As Solomos and Back (1996, pp. 18–19) explain, much of what was once identified as 'race' is now coded as 'culture', retaining a sense of fixity but losing the explicit connection to genetic inheritance; what is often dubbed new 'cultural racism'. Yet culture is also a complex and slippery idea, referring to whole 'ways of life' and to 'sub'-cultures within those 'wholes'; to what seem to be fixed and bounded communities and to dynamic and situated processes of group formation; to high art and to popular culture; to 'ethnically' defined groups and to questions of class, gender and so on (Jenks, 1993).

'Ethnicity' might seem to narrow this array, and it might seem to avoid the problems of race, but it is no less troubled. At one level ethnicity simply refers to a sense of commonality based on several characteristics: language, physical similarities, national origin, customs, religion and so on. Yet ethnicity is often used to denote a primordial identity just as 'deep' as race. Ethnicity is, in fact, a social construction based on the perception of these shared qualities, borne out of the interaction between self-identification and identification by others (Bottomley, 1979; Brubaker, 2004). It can sometimes be an absurd construction based on an amalgam of categories. A key UK document reviewing the research on ethnicity and education for the Department of Education and Skills (DfES, 2006), for example, used the following 'Ethnicity codes': 'White' and 'Black' (i.e. colour or 'race'), Asian and African (continents), Pakistani and Chinese (country), 'mixed' and 'British' (whatever they refer to). The idea of 'Asian', for example, as we have indicated, is problematic because it includes a range of diverse nations, languages, religions, classes and urban and rural settings, and, in any case, means different things in different nations. Indeed, when we turn to the links between educational outcomes and ethnicity, Windle (2004, pp. 276–7) argues that analytical categories of 'ethnicity' have no unified meaning outside of their relation to conditions of arrival and settlement, economic and political climate, and so on.

In Australia, most 'ethnicities' are in fact forms of nation-based identification that, as a result of migration, collapse an array of differences into a homogenizing category; that is, it is a contextually specific and dynamic process of drawing boundaries and asserting identities which involves complex relation to notions of culture, nation and race (Brah, 1996). Being 'Chinese' in China is a project of national imagining: in Australia it becomes an 'ethnicity'. Moreover, 'ethnic' is a term that is colloquially applied in Australia to those peoples with a LBOTE rather than an Anglo or ESB, as if being 'Anglo-Saxon' or 'Anglo-Celtic' did not constitute an ethnicity. The shorthand 'Anglo' is the term of identification used here that groups together long-time Australians of ESB. In an Australian context it is used more regularly than the racial category 'white' and is preferable to the common but problematic use of 'Australian' which is simply a category of nationality. However, because 'ethnic' has developed negative connotations in Australia, it has become increasingly common to refer to 'cultures'.

Talk about 'cultures' doesn't solve the problem of terminology, however, because 'culture' refers to a whole array of processes beyond ethnicity. Moreover, once we turn it into a noun – a culture – we end up with the same problems of seeing culture or ethnicity as a *thing* not a multidimensional, relational *process*. The point here is not to offer a better definition of these terms, but to recognize the *complexity* at the heart of what we are talking about when we invoke notions of ethnicity or culture (Noble, 2011; Watkins, 2011a). People exist at the intersection of multiple social processes and to reduce them to a single, innate 'culture' loses this complexity. The forms of communal life we identify as 'cultures' are not primordial categories but the result of particular kinds of *practices*, which relate to social relations and institutions and develop over time. These points don't detract from the important ways people identify with a particular ethnicity, but suggest that when we use categories of ethnicity, as we do here, we are referring not to analytical categories based on fixed and bounded groups, but descriptive categories based on forms of identification. This means that ethnicity becomes a way into studying complex educational and social practices, not a way of categorizing or explaining them in a reductive fashion (Brah, 1996; Nasir and Saxe, 2003).

From psychological attributes to embodied capacities

A central aim of this book is to explore those practices which aid participation in schooling, and to see these in terms of patterns of ethnicity; not to confirm cultural pathologies but to open up our analysis of complex practices. To do this we will use several concepts – educational capital, disposition and habitus – that derive from the work of Pierre Bourdieu. Bourdieu examines the role of schools in the reproduction of cultural capital – the learned competence in the valued ways of doing things – as the 'consecration' of class-based knowledge and power (Bourdieu and Passeron, 1990). He later acknowledged the productive nature of this competence (Bourdieu, 1996) and we use the term 'educational capital' to cover the array of competencies, skills and knowledges that serve these functions within the schooling system. These competencies are distributed unevenly, according to ethnicity, SES and gender, but are not reducible to the reproduction of power. Moreover, they form the basis of students' *dispositions* towards learning.

A significant body of research – particularly in the field of educational psychology – has drawn attention to the fact that educational performance is linked to specific dispositions towards learning. Educational success corresponds to dispositions which entail high levels of motivation and aspiration, self-efficacy and self-regulation, achievement orientation and a desire to learn, diligence, and so on (McInerney and Van Etten, 2001; Lamb et al., 2004). While useful, much of this research tends to derive broad generalizations from large surveys, slipping from the personal attributes of individuals to features of ethnically defined groups. Further, because these dispositions are framed as psychological attributes, this literature seems to confirm assumptions that they are rooted in deep-seated and unchanging cultural pathologies. Little research grapples with such dispositions in empirical contexts, which could help to explore the extent to which they are interactive and dynamic entities (Bloomer and Hodkinson, 2000, p. 589). This book argues that the emphasis on psychological attributes in this research often means that it overlooks the ways these capacities derive from particular practices endorsed in the home and school environments in which a child operates.

Rather than locate these dispositions in some innate qualities of the learner or their ethnic background, we want to see them as specific *capacities* and forms of *educational capital* that emerge from specific *practices*. Against the cognitive and psychological orientations in educational research, we want to suggest that educational participation depends on particular embodied capacities which are evidence of *dispositions towards learning* which, in turn, affect cognitive ability. The mastery of certain skills, behaviours and knowledges is what we call, drawing on the work of Bourdieu, the *scholarly habitus* (Watkins, 2005a, 2011b). By examining this we can better understand the relationships between ethnic background and educational performance.

This does not just involve the ability to perform certain tasks but the desire to learn and the ability to manage one's learning. We address these issues not by pathologizing ethnicity nor by extrapolating backwards to make some claim about prior cultural values, but by exploring the ways educational capital is internalized by students in ways that dispose them towards, or away from, educational achievement. We deploy the notion of a scholarly habitus to analyse the development of these dispositions through practices that underlie the capacity for educational success. Bourdieu uses the concept of 'habitus' to describe the embodied dispositions which make it possible for someone to function appropriately and largely unconsciously in a particular milieu: a set of durable thoughts and actions through which our history is internalized (Bourdieu, 1990, p. 53). Bourdieu was primarily interested in considering the role of the habitus in the reproduction of class relations by legitimizing the cultural capital of the powerful. This book will argue that it is important to examine embodied capacities not simply as forms of social reproduction, but as the grounds of socially powerful dispositions to learning.

The bodily basis to educational participation is generally ignored in educational research, except in the specific areas of physical education and health (Evans, 2004; Wright, 2004). When it has been examined, the focus has been on education as a form of bodily control (Goodson and Dowbiggin,

1990; Gore, 1998; Prout, 2000; Besley and Peters, 2007). Instead, this book will think of discipline as potentially enabling (Watkins, 2005a, 2011b). This draws on a reading of Foucault's work, which acknowledges the productive capacity of discipline, but ultimately focuses more on practices of domination and surveillance that produce 'docile' bodies than on 'useful' bodies that have capacities that enable them to work effectively in a given setting (Foucault, 1977). Such discipline is partially taught in the early years of school, but is more likely to be assumed as the 'natural' propensity of the successful learner. The acquisition of this discipline needs close examination particularly as it pertains to different ethnic groups and sociocultural backgrounds. Research, for example, into parenting practices in various nations would suggest that ethnicity might impact on students' motivational orientation, but only through *specific* practices (Choo and Tan, 2001; Strom, 2001; Campbell and Verna, 2007). These studies show that a relation between ethnicity and productive practices exists, but that any simple claim about 'Asian values', for example, is misplaced.

The concept of a scholarly habitus is useful then in exploring the links between home and school practices, embodied dispositions and sociocultural background because it allows us to address issues of self-regulation and the possession of educational capital without falling into simplistic arguments about 'ethnic drive'. Moreover, it allows us to shift the focus from test results to questions about the dispositions that shape performance, and from discipline as classroom management, punishment and the supposed better ethos of elite schools, to capacities for self-direction that have implications for the educational opportunities of students. This books aims to foster insights into these issues by considering whether:

- there is evidence of different dispositions to learning among specific ethnic groups and if these are critical to academic achievement;

- these dispositions are related to knowledge of the schooling system and home-based practices such as routines around homework, workspace, parental regulation and extracurricular activities;

- different practices relate to family experiences, SES and, to some extent, gender[2] as well as ethnicity;

- classroom practices promote bodily dispositions conducive to academic endeavour.

These questions have practical consequences. How we perceive the differential achievement of students from different ethnic backgrounds shapes both educational policy and classroom practices. It is important, therefore, that the book is framed by a consideration of the perceptions of the relationship between ethnicity and education, both through wider social debates and as the specific professional vision of teachers.

Researching ethnicity, schooling and the scholarly habitus

This book draws on research into the dispositions to learning of Year 3 students (aged 8/9 years) from Chinese, Pasifika and Anglo backgrounds in primary schools in Sydney, Australia. The rationale for a focus on Year 3 students lies in the significance of this year within Australian state-based education systems. Year 3 is the first year in which all students across Australia undertake nation-wide tests for literacy and numeracy. This type of test data provides a useful measure of each student's achievement and additional comparative information on the schools involved in the study.[3] Also, in their following year, students may sit for tests for admission to selective classes for Years 5 and 6. Responses to questions about these tests provided useful insights into students' performance and their own and their parents' educational aspirations. Year 3 is also important as it represents the first year of primary school with students having already completed three years of infants school. Dispositions to learning are evident by this stage of a student's school life but they are not as engrained as is generally the case by the end of primary school, prior to their entry to high school (Watkins, 2011). Given these factors it was felt that Year 3 was an optimal time to investigate a student's dispositions to learning and the ways in which both home and school had contributed to their formation.

Students from Chinese, Pasifika and Anglo backgrounds were chosen for inclusion in the study due to public perceptions of their academic achievement. As discussed, students of Chinese background are seen as high achievers while those of Pasifika backgrounds are generally viewed as low achievers. Typically, Anglo students are not seen in ethnic nor educationally cohesive terms, and so make a useful comparison. Each of the categories – Chinese, Pasifika and Anglo – were extrapolated from the forms of self-identification that parents provided in a survey which contained an expression of interest for their child to be involved in the interview and observation components of the study. Although we use the category of 'Chinese', this is shorthand for a range of different ancestries that respondents nominated, such as Chinese, Chinese-Australian, Hong-Kong Chinese, Taiwanese-Australian. This is also the case with 'Pasifika' which is used to denote participants from Samoan, Tongan, Cook Islander, Māori, Fijian and Tokelauan backgrounds. The majority of participants termed 'Pasifika', however, had either a Samoan or Tongan heritage. The third category 'Anglo' includes those who identified as Anglo,

Anglo-Australian, Anglo-Saxon, Anglo-Celt or Australian. It is a term that has considerable currency in Australia. Country of birth and language background were also used to enable categorization in terms of these three broad groups with the understanding that, while each had a degree of coherence, there was also considerable internal variation. As we indicate, these terms are descriptive categories designed to provide ways into analysing educational processes, bouncing off social perceptions of difference, not prescriptive terms indicating causality.

The project also gave some attention to the SES and gender of students in an attempt to more fully understand the complexity of cultural difference. In all, there were 11 Chinese students, eight boys and three girls with five from backgrounds of middle to high SES and six of a low SES.[4] There were also 11 Pasifika students, seven boys and four girls, with all these students from low SES backgrounds. Lastly, there were 13 Anglo students, eight boys and five girls with five from middle to high SES backgrounds and eight from low SES backgrounds. The students involved in the study attended one of six schools that were selected in terms of their populations of Chinese, Pasifika and Anglo students. Schools were grouped in the following ways: Group 1 included two schools with high populations of Chinese students; Group 2 included two schools with high populations of Pasifika students and Group 3 included two schools with a reasonable representation of each of these two groups. As the schools with high percentages of Chinese students tended to be of a higher SES than those with large populations of Pasifika students, the rationale behind selecting schools for inclusion in Group 3 was to try and minimize this imbalance. A number of Anglo students were selected from across the three groups of schools. A profile of each of the schools and the names and ethnicity of students involved in the study is given in Table 0.1.

Rather than simply adopting the methods associated with traditional social science research, such as large-scale surveys and structured interviews, which were unable to capture the experience of the different students we were investigating, we adopted what Johnson et al. (2004, p. 26) refer to as 'methodological pluralism' that was used within a framework of cultural research (Ang, 2005). This involved a range of techniques, both qualitative and quantitative, with the potential to shed light on the diversity within each of the groups of students under investigation, which, while indicating a common ethnicity, varied internally in terms of their class, religion, education, previous experience and duration in Australia. This diversity is also characteristic of the various 'cultures of schooling' encountered within each site as the six schools involved in the study varied considerably in terms of the pedagogies their teachers employed and emphasis each placed on such things as the academic and pastoral dimensions of schooling. The study drew on data from several sources – a survey, in-depth interviews, observation and document analysis – to attain a triangulation of data, but not as it is understood within

TABLE 0.1 School profiles[5]

Group 1 schools	
Chestervale Public School (PS)	**Colinville PS**
Chestervale PS is located in a middle-SES suburb in Sydney's north-west with an overall population of 700 students. Chinese background students, from mainly Hong Kong, China and Malaysia, make up 74% of the student population. The school has an Anglo population of 12%. The remaining major ethnic groups are Indian and Korean.	Colinville PS also has a population of 700 students including Opportunity Classes in Years 5 and 6. It is located in an inner-western suburb of Sydney and, while there are a considerable number of students whose parents have professional and managerial employment backgrounds, there are also some from a lower SES. The school is 55% LBOTE with significant numbers from Chinese backgrounds.
Chestervale PS students involved in the study:	**Colinville PS students involved in the study:**
Chinese background – Ben, Jenny, Walter and Norman	Chinese background – Alice, Gary, Yupeng and Seamus
Anglo background – Wallace, Eric and Ian	Anglo background – Flynn and Melissa
Group 2 schools	
Allerton PS	**Aston PS**
Allerton PS is a school of 400 students located in the south-western suburbs of Sydney in an area of considerable disadvantage. Most students' families live in public housing accommodation and the school receives extra government funding. Allerton PS is approximately 60% LBOTE with half of these students of Pasifika background, mainly Samoan. The student population is also 8% Aboriginal.	Aston PS with a student population of 500 is located in the outer-western suburbs of Sydney. Most families are of a low SES and the school receives extra government funding. The largest group within the LBOTE population is Pasifika, mainly Samoan, though there are also Cook Islander, Tongan and Māori students at the school. In addition to this, 23% of the population is Aboriginal. Given the relatively transient nature of the Pasifika population in the area, there were considerable difficulties in recruiting Pasifika students for the study.
Allerton PS students involved in the study:	**Aston PS students involved in the study:**
Pasifika background – Darren, Joe, Lottie and Tuilia	Pasifika background – Tim

TABLE 0.1 Continued

Anglo background – Bryon and Tilly	Anglo background – Braydon, Leanne and Narelle
Group 3 schools	
Broughton Heights PS	**Briar Plains PS**
Broughton Heights is a very large school of over 1,000 students. Located in the western suburbs of Sydney it draws on families from lower-middle and low-SES backgrounds. There was a range of different ethnic groups represented at the school with students of Chinese background being approximately 50% and Pasifika students 9% (mainly Tongan and Samoan). Other backgrounds represented at the school include Lebanese, Iraqi, Afghani, Sudanese, Vietnamese and Korean.	Briar Plains PS is also located in the western suburbs of Sydney and draws on a similar population to Broughton Heights PS. Its student population is 550 with 98% being LBOTE. Of these, 19% are of Pasifika background, 38% Arabic-speaking and 6% Chinese. There are very few Anglo students at the school.
Broughton Heights PS students involved in the study:	**Briar Plains PS students involved in the study:**
Chinese background – Sonya and Vincent	Chinese background – Robbie
Pasifika background – Sonny, Finau and Fred	Pasifika background – Emma, Lua and Toni
Anglo background – Joan and Callum	Anglo background – Jason

a more traditional research paradigm as a technique for obtaining a verifiable truth. Rather, by employing multiple methods, in particular the interviews and classroom observations, a perspective on the richly textured nature of the participants' experience provided understandings about the differential achievement of students from different ethnic backgrounds.

The study was undertaken in two phases. Firstly, there was a survey of all parents of Year 3 students in ten primary schools within the Sydney metropolitan area. This was followed by interviews, observations and analysis of relevant policies and curriculum material in six of these schools, as well as ongoing media analysis. The purpose of the survey was to amass broad data on attitudes and practices around learning at home and school and to select the final group of six schools and the parents and students to be involved in the second phase of the study.[6] Parents of all 11 Chinese and 13 Anglo students and those of 10 of the 11 Pasifika parents were interviewed. Together with this, interviews were also held with each of the students' teachers, the school principals and deputies, English as a Second Language (ESL) teachers, Chinese, Tongan and Samoan community liaison officers and other community representatives were interviewed. In all 105 interviews were conducted. The interview questions for parents and students were based around similar questions presented in the survey with more specific treatment of habits and practices in the home, extracurricular activities and aspirations. The questions for teachers centred on classroom practices and possible observed differences between groups of students, behaviour, self-regulation and engagement. The school executive and community representatives were questioned on issues related to school and community relations, parental involvement, school ethos, discipline and homework policies, and the achievement levels of different groups of students.

In addition to the survey and interview data, the study drew on observation in each child's classroom and school, and within their homes which was essential for investigating the practices in which students engaged; the forms of discipline which shaped their bodies and the dispositions to learning that these promote. The aim of the observation sessions was to capture what was happening in each of the Year 3 classrooms in relation to the participating students, other students (especially those from the ethnicities foregrounded in the study), the class overall and interaction between teacher and students. Observations also recorded the use of the pedagogic space, classroom regimen and curriculum implementation (Watkins, 2011b). The number of observation sessions per class ranged from two to four, and were observed by two of three researchers on separate occasions.

Organization of the book

This wealth of data from various sources assisted in attaining a detailed account of the experience of the students in the three groups. Each chapter draws on different aspects of this data. Chapter 1 provides a scene-setting exploration of the media representation of the educational performance of Chinese and Pasifika students within Australia and other migrant ESB nations. It demonstrates the ethnicization of academic achievement in Australian debates, the ways in which media debates rest on reified conceptions of ethnicity to 'explain' educational success or failure fuelling public perceptions. This chapter lays the groundwork for the claim that it is social practices, not cultural pathologies, which are the basis for understanding the links between ethnicity and academic performance.

Chapter 2 focuses on the issue of educational capital, the various resources individuals accumulate – forms of knowledge, skills, values, qualifications and so on – which shape practices around academic engagement within the home and children's performance at school. Drawing primarily on survey data, it provides some initial insights into the relationships between parents' ethnicity, their educational capital, home practices, students' experiences at school and their dispositions to learning. Chapter 3 moves from perceptions to practices, drawing together some of the empirical data to demonstrate the existence of specific dispositions towards learning among the different groups of students. It uses the classroom observations and interviews with students, parents and teachers to examine attitudes to schooling, aspirations, expectations and classroom behaviour, and links this to test results, to make some general claims about the evidence for specific dispositions among students and their relation to patterns of ethnicity.

Central to this book is the argument that the scholarly habitus cannot be explained away by pathologies of ethnicity or SES, but has to be examined in terms of the practices which produce these capacities. In Chapter 4, we consider key practices within the home, such as routines associated with homework, participation in extracurricular activities and parents' encouragement of their child's educational work as a way of examining how the dispositions discussed in Chapter 3 may be produced. Chapter 5 shifts to the school and examines teachers' and students' perceptions and attitudes to learning; whether teachers feel students of particular ethnic backgrounds favour certain pedagogic approaches and contrasts this with the views of the students. Chapter 6 continues the examination of teaching and learning, exploring the ways in which school cultures and classroom practices engender forms of discipline that contribute to different dispositions to learning. This is undertaken through an examination of the classroom experiences of a selection of the students from Chinese, Pasifika and Anglo backgrounds, including an analysis of the organization and regimen of their classrooms and the techniques their teachers employ in implementing the curriculum. The book concludes with a summary of the key arguments around the links between ethnicity and dispositions to learning and discusses the consequences for teaching and research. It reasserts the importance of a focus on practice in analysing the relationship between ethnicity and education and how the acquisition of a scholarly habitus is fundamental to the academic success of students, no matter what their background.

1

The ethnicization of educational achievement

Multicultural education in Australia dates back to the late 1960s, when a number of changes in curriculum began to transform the ways schools approached the needs of LBOTE students (Inglis, 2009, p. 111). Under the previous Child Migrant Education Program, the education of the 'migrant child' was framed primarily as a problem of them 'fitting in', with an emphasis on the learning of English and conforming to Australian ways (Martin, 1978, pp. 84, 89). With the formalization of multicultural education during the 1970s, the provision of ESL tuition to recently arrived LBOTE migrants remained the mainstay, but multicultural education increasingly encompassed a diverse range of policies and programmes around anti-racism, multicultural perspectives across the curriculum, community liaison, inclusive curriculum and community languages.

The educational attempt to address the diverse goals of multiculturalism in a rapidly changing society is a remarkable story, but this is not the focus of this book. The initial point here is the transformation of language that multiculturalism brings to the understanding of schooling. 'Ethnicity' emerges as a key category of social and educational discourse. It replaces an emphasis on the 'migrant', as language and culture mark differences among new arrivals (Martin, 1978, p. 16), and an earlier language of 'race', increasingly discredited as a category and, in any case, associated with a white colonial past and an indigenous population (Allan and Hill, 2004, p. 980). But ethnicity is not simply something everyone has; in Australia it comes to be equated with particular LBOTE migrants. Those from southern and eastern Europe, the Middle East and Asia are more likely to be identified as 'ethnics' and, because this becomes in effect a pejorative term, it too is conflated with and eventually replaced by 'culture', as a softer but more complex term. Ethnicity – or culture – comes to rival socio-economic disadvantage as a central determinant of educational performance. Indeed, some scholars argue that ethnicity replaces class as the key category of educational disadvantage (Foster and Stockley, 1984, p. 9).

Most significantly, in a social context of demographic changes associated with changing migration patterns, the educational needs of children with a LBOTE were not simply technical problems to do with the acquisition of English, but were linked to a broader set of issues to do with the cultural background of students and their families (Martin, 1978, p. 132). This set of concerns, however, was focused primarily on poorly performing students. In this sense, multicultural education derived from a perceived deficit: the idea that immigrant children entering Australian schools lacked the linguistic and cultural competence to succeed academically. While of course there was some truth to this, the problem was that this often amounted to a reductive equation of ethnicity *with* educational disadvantage. Ethnicity was linked directly and necessarily to poor educational outcomes. It then became a category of disadvantage and the role of multicultural education was to address this injustice. Together, this change amounted to the *ethnicization* of educational disadvantage. Drawing on the literature on racialization, ethnicization here refers to the 'ways of seeing' social phenomena that privilege questions of ethnicity, entailing a dynamic relation between social perceptions of difference and socio-structural relations through which particular kinds of complex social problems come to be seen in 'ethnic' terms (Collins et al., 2000, p. 18; Murji and Solomos, 2005, pp. 13–14). Some scholars argued not just that ethnicity became a key category of disadvantage, but that this operated as an ideological masking of key structural features of inequality (de Lepervanche, 1980).

As indicated in the Introduction, the relationship between ethnicity and education outcomes is complicated. There is no simple causal relation, but a range of patterns (Noble and Poynting, 2000). Today, while the performance of some LBOTE students is still well below that of their ESB peers, such as those of Arabic-speaking and various Pasifika backgrounds, it is no longer the case for many who have an Asian background. Students of Mandarin and Cantonese speaking backgrounds in particular consistently outperform ESB students in Australian national testing programmes.[1] Ethnicity, especially as it has been understood in Australia, can no longer be equated with educational disadvantage. Rather, particular 'ethnicities', especially those that might be termed 'Chinese' appear to have an educational *ad*vantage. This academic success is not unique to children of the Australian Chinese diaspora; it is a phenomenon evident elsewhere with Chinese-background students regularly topping school assessment and university entrance exams internationally (e.g. Canada: Hammer and Friesen, 2011; New Zealand: Cumming, 2011; United Kingdom: Disley, 2011; United States: Reed, 2011). Yet, instead of viewing this success in a positive way as an indication of the ease with which many Chinese students have adapted to Western systems of schooling, more often than not, it attracts negative media attention playing on public anxieties around how 'Chinese success' might reflect upon the performance of the 'Anglo' majority, the Australian schooling system or, indeed, upon multiculturalism. This chapter explores the way perceptions of ethnic difference are constructed by the media, in particular the various rationales presented for the outstanding performance of many Chinese students in Australia and other Western migrant nations. It contrasts this with media representation of Pasifika students in Australia and New Zealand which tends to highlight their much lower achievement rates. What this reveals is a broader ethnicization of educational achievement, more expansive than early multiculturalism's ethnicization of disadvantage. Central to these processes is a problematic way of seeing ethnicity, or culture, as fixed and bounded. Exploring this issue is important because, as the book will argue, if ethnicity itself is seen as determining a child's performance at school then this gets in the way of a more systematic and productive analysis of the formation of habits of learning acquired within the home and at school and their uneven distribution.

Tiger mothers and 'Chinese success'

Public anxiety over 'Chinese success' was nowhere more evident than in the international media coverage following the release of Amy Chua's *Battle Hymn of the Tiger Mother* in the United States in January 2011. In this memoir-cum-parenting guide, Chua slams Western parenting techniques and links the impressive academic and all-round performance of Chinese students to their strict upbringing. Chua, born in the United States of Chinese-born parents who came to the United States from the Philippines, uses the book to detail her own upbringing. Now a Yale law professor, Chua also recounts her experiences as a Chinese Tiger Mother enforcing rigid study routines and music practice upon her two daughters, both A grade students and, despite some resistance from her younger daughter, musical prodigies. Chua frames the different parenting philosophies of the East and West, and tensions that arise over these in her household, as a 'bitter clash of cultures'. With allusions to Huntington's 'clash of civilisations', this 'clash of cultures' astutely targets that which is most sacred to parents – their children (Huntington, 1997). It plays on Western parents' anxieties over wanting to do the best by their children. Chua contrasts what she sees as the laxity of Western parents with the strict disciplinary approach of the Chinese. She claims there are numerous studies that confirm these differences, discussing one in which 70 per cent of Western mothers feel stressing academic success is not good for children and that emphasis needs to be placed on the idea that 'learning is fun'. In comparison,

Chua (2011, p. 5) indicates that 'roughly none' of the Chinese immigrant mothers in the study were of this view and neither is Chua, who elaborates this difference in her discussion of her own parenting style. The anxieties of Western parents, however, are put at ease as Chua comes to question the 'Tiger Mother' approach, given her younger daughter's reaction to the pressure. This admission, and the concessions Chua then affords her daughter, provides some reassurance that Western parenting may have its benefits.

Reaction to Chua's memoir was overwhelming. Prior to its publication, the *Wall Street Journal* released an excerpt with the headline 'Why Chinese mothers are superior' which was read by over one million readers and attracted 7,000 comments within a fortnight (Paul, 2011). As the book provoked vigorous debate about parenting styles, much of it critical of Chua's treatment of her daughters, it soon escalated into a national debate within the United States about China's threat to America's global dominance. In its front page coverage, *Time Magazine* also took this angle declaring that, 'Chinese parenting has hit hard at a national sore spot: our fears about losing ground to China . . . and about adequately preparing our children to survive in the global economy' (Paul, 2011). US parenting was criticized as too soft. It claimed that Western parents were more concerned about their children's psyche and self-esteem than disciplining them appropriately (Gibbs, 2011; Luscombe, 2011). Significantly, Chua's book was published shortly after the release of the 2009 Organization for Economic Development and Cooperation (OECD) Programme for International Student Assessment (PISA) results in which Shanghai students, in their first year of undertaking the tests, were ranked number one while the United States was seventeenth. There was a feeling that Chua may not only have exposed problems with parenting but weaknesses in the US education system. With a focus on Confucian values of respect for authority and a prizing of education, Chinese students were said to work harder and for longer hours. Commenting on the PISA results, President Obama even suggested they represented a 'Sputnik Moment', a wake-up call to America to rethink its approach to education (Paul, 2011).

Reaction to Chua's book was not confined to the United States but sparked debate internationally. In Western migrant nations like Australia, the United Kingdom, Canada and New Zealand, media coverage replicated that of the United States but with some modification for different national agendas. But it was a debate that was often played out at a local level. Its global reach is illustrated, for example, by the response of the *Northern District Times* (*NDT*), a local newspaper in Epping, a northern suburb of Sydney, Australia with a large Chinese population.[2] While Australian television news, current affairs programmes and metropolitan newspapers all reported reaction to the book, the *NDT* sought a local angle, particularly given two of the top selective high schools in the state education system were located in the area. With the headline, 'Are Chinese Kids Smarter?', it called on readers to 'cast their vote' on the newspaper website, to which 78 per cent of responses were 'yes' (Freymark, 2011, p. 1; *NDT*, 2012). In the setting up of an opposition between 'east and west cultures', the newspaper seemed attuned to Anglo anxiety regarding the large numbers of students from Chinese backgrounds in the area's selective schools at the expense of those from an Anglo background. To shed light on the matter the paper sought the opinion of the principal of a local Chinese community language school, herself a 'mother of two'. Taking the middle ground, the principal indicated that while 'Westerners' could learn from 'the Chinese' in terms of their focus on hard work, basic skills and involvement in their children's education, she felt 'Western people make children stronger by encouraging strength from the inside', alluding to a supposed Western focus on psychological well-being over the pressure Chinese parents exerted on their children to succeed academically (Freymark, 2011, p. 1). The principal added that Chinese parents at her school felt she 'should push the children harder' (Freymark, 2011, p. 1).

Central to the Tiger Mother debates is the uncritical and reductive language of ethnic and cultural categories, especially in terms of the coherence of what it means to *be* Chinese. In positing a radical difference between 'east and west cultures', 'culture' is framed as something one is born with rather than what is acquired over time and space, and something one never relinquishes; a monolithic category resistant to change, with firm boundaries around what constitutes one culture and another, fostering an 'us' and 'them' mentality: 'east' and 'west', 'Chinese' and 'American' or 'Australian'. The 'cultures' of diasporic communities are seen as remaining in tact, impervious to the day-to-day interactions and modes of being negotiated by individuals in their newfound home. Despite the principal quoted in the *NDT* having lived in Australia for 21 years, she is still seen as essentially Chinese and it is this which grants her the authority to confirm Chua's demarcation of a clear cultural difference between Australian and Chinese approaches to parenting.

Chua is similarly identified as Chinese, referred to in the *NDT* as a 'Chinese Professor' and 'American-based' rather than American-born. This identification resists any complexity about the category 'Chinese' and sustains the simple pitting of culture against culture; the bitter clash Chua claims in her book. Yet, in her opening chapter Chua provides some qualification as to what she means by a 'Chinese Mother'. She insists they need not be Chinese at all and appears to use the expression as a metaphor for a mother who employs strict parenting techniques. She even points out the term may not apply to all mothers of Chinese heritage, though adds if this is the case, they are 'almost always born in the West' (Chua, 2011, p. 4). These qualifications, however, are unsustained and carry little weight. As Chua declares herself both 'Chinese' and a 'Tiger Mother', this coupling of categories belies the nuances.

The foregrounding of 'Chineseness' in this debate happens in several ways. First, while there are occasional references to students from other Asian nations, by and large the performance of students and their parents from these nations is backgrounded. Second, Chineseness is drained of the complex ethnic, linguistic, religious, class, regional and urban/rural differences that mark China as a country. Further, the complexities of being a Malay or Philippine Chinese, or coming from Hong Kong or Taiwan are left out of the equation (though, as we will see, 'Chinese' frequently expands to become 'Asian' at strategic moments). As with any form of identification denoting ethnicity or nationality, the category 'Chinese' is not a singular or uniform identity, even if it is used to denote such a thing. As Ang (2001, p. 38) points out, there are 'many different Chinese identities not one'. Ladegaard (2012), for example, explains how Chinese students from Hong Kong and Mainland China tend to use very different identity markers, often to differentiate themselves from the other, though this is contingent on a range of shifting and situated factors. Yet, as with ethnocultural identities in general there is a tendency to essentialize, of which Chua herself is guilty, though, with an eye to the market, this is perhaps strategically employed. These forms of reduction and conflation are crucial to the process of ethnicization, but they are not enough. In a kind of metonymic transfer, particular practices are simply equated with being Chinese and constitutive of Chinese culture. As Clark and Gieve (2006) argue, the construction of 'the Chinese learner' is premised on a 'large culture' approach, which involves describing the values, attitudes and practices of individuals in terms of fixed, homogeneous, reified national cultures.

The ethnic othering of 'the Chinese'

Ethnicity is only one dimension of identity. Among other things, class, gender, religion and family need to be acknowledged, yet in discussion of academic performance, it is ethnicity that is often foregrounded. To an Anglo white majority that is not cognizant of its own ethnicity, it is this marker of difference that assumes significance in trying to find explanations for 'non-normative' performance – be it high, as in the case of the Chinese, or low, as with Pasifika students. As Ahmed (2004, p. 1) suggests, for Anglos, their 'whiteness' is invisible, 'the non-colour, the absent present or hidden referent, against which all other colours are measured as forms of deviance'. Deviant behaviour generally refers to that which is negative, to be seen as inferior. Yet the Chinese 'deviance' relates to something positive, performing *too* well, beating the Anglos at their own game, excelling in subjects across the curriculum – even English – once the preserve of native speakers. In the portrayal of Chinese success, difference becomes deviation from the norm and thence pathological deviance.

This success is negativized through the media preoccupation with the supposed consequences of the Chinese work ethic: the psychological harm due to over work, the loss of childhood by limiting play, the rise in suicide from increased anxiety and a focus on conformity over creativity through excessive drill. In constructing this as a form of social deviance, it is necessary to assign the homogenized category of 'Chinese' particular traits, to fashion them as radically Other, and then to pathologize them. One strategy is the testimonial, the 'insider account' from Chinese students of the effects of placing too much emphasis on academic success. The *NDT* made use of one of their young cadet reporters, Jingwen Sun, an international student who had been living in Australia for four and a half years, to provide insights into how Chinese students 'are driven to success at school' (Sun, 2011, p. 2). She reports on how she was fortunate to be a 'good' student willing 'to study a lot, up to five hours extra in high school rather than be forced to by her parents'. She also adds that she knows 'there are parents who force their children to study more and more' (Sun, 2011, p. 2). Similar accounts appeared in newspapers internationally following the release of Chua's book. In New Zealand, for example, Chloe Lau, a Year 12 student of Chinese background 'urges Asian parents to lighten up on the pressure' explaining how 'It is common knowledge that Asian parents can often be manipulative and domineering' (Lau, 2011). After migrating from China, 17-year-old Kyle Yu told Canada's *Globe and Mail* that he felt, 'In China, his job is to study, in Canada his job is to learn' (Hammer and Friesen, 2011, http://global.factiva.com.ezproxy.uws.edu.au/ha/default.aspx). In the United States, Mon-Shane Chou, a 19-year-old student at Pasadena City College commented that 'being raised in a strict, high pressure household is psychologically damaging' (Oldham, 2011).

The *NDT* also sought the opinion of Chinese mothers in the local area. Coverage on reaction to Chua's book spanned three weeks! In the third instalment reported in the 'Golden Tiger', a special weekly section designed for Chinese readers, five mothers presented their views. Under the headline 'Tiger Mum Amy under Fire', a photograph of each of the women appeared with their name and a comment on Chua's perspective on parenting. While most saw some benefit in 'Chinese-style' parenting in the early years, they were generally critical of Chua's techniques and focused on the importance of 'balance'. Forgotten in all the hype is how Chua also settled on a 'hybrid approach' (Chua, 2011, p. 225). Given that the reservations of these potential Tiger Mums do not refute the veracity of Chua's take on Chinese parenting, they simply justify Anglo concerns that these practices are in fact both 'Chinese' and damaging to children. Of course stories also emerged in praise of Chinese parenting and Chua's own daughters admit they were pleased their mother forced them to practise and study hard. Some reports taking a more positive stance simply see Chua as a caricature exaggerating the negative for effect, focusing 'on the pathological end of the Chinese mother spectrum' (McMahon, 2011, p. 3). Other reports claim such a hardline approach and strict routines simply didn't do any harm. In the *Time* article 'An American Dad Raising a Tiger Daughter', Bill Powell, married to a Chinese woman and living in Shanghai, assures readers that despite his 6-year-old, American passport-holding daughter having a very busy schedule involving violin and ballet lessons, 2–3 hours homework a night seven days a week and her mother drilling her each night in math and Chinese, that 'she's a normal kid' (Powell, 2011). Defending his child's normality, *despite* these routines, effectively encourages the perception that such approaches to parenting are problematic. Distinct from Western norms of parenting that draw on romantic notions of childhood innocence and play, such practices are simply viewed as deviant. One of the many blog posts on the *Time Magazine* website, for example, laments the 'incurable loss of childhood'. Julia Baird (2011, p. 11) employs a similar technique in critiquing the Tiger Mother approach in her *Sydney Morning Herald* column, explaining that,

> Hordes of expats move back to Australia from countries where academic competition is intense, knowing that running barefoot under big blazing blue skies can bring an unsurpassed joy to childhood. If we would just applaud the pursuit of academic excellence as loudly as we applaud the pursuit of goals and wickets we could be certain we are giving our children a chance to live life to the fullest: by inspiring them, not beating them into submission.

Despite a criticism of what she sees as the valorization of sport in Australia over academic pursuits, Baird finds a focus on academic competition during childhood as problematic. As Jackson and Scott (1999, p. 86) detail in their discussion of the social construction of childhood, it is a period portrayed as 'a precious realm under siege from those who would rob children of their childhood'. From this perspective, an emphasis on routine and drill to promote study habits is 'unnatural'; an imposition upon young children who should be free to play and experience the world unfettered. Yet, such a view essentializes the desire to learn assuming, as does Baird, that academic endeavour is simply a matter of inspiration rather than linked to an assemblage of skills that habit and routine can engender. Baird instead characterizes such processes as 'beating them into submission', providing the argument, designed to ease Anglo anxiety over Chinese success, that commitment to academic endeavour is only achieved at the expense of a student's childhood. Arguments such as these are replayed over and over again in the media producing a kind of moral panic wherein, 'Rather than private anxieties informing public debates, public debates structure private anxieties' (Critcher, 2003, p. 163). Anglo parents are provided with a certain rationale for what they might see as the displacement of their own children in selective schools, yet one which offers them a certain satisfaction that they are doing the right thing by their children in not pushing them 'like the Chinese'. It is significant that these practices are characterized as distinctively 'Chinese', ignoring the intensive studying and practice that academically (and musically) successful children of any background have often undertaken.

Further justification of the view that (Chinese) parental pressure to perform is psychologically damaging is the purported excessive suicide rates among Chinese youth. In Australia, one report pointed out that 'Conspicuously absent from Chua's memoir is any mention of how young Asian-American women, who often struggle to meet their parents' expectations, suffer abnormally high suicide rates' (Neill, 2011). Yet another refers to how Chua 'does not mention China's shocking rate of youth suicide' (Rowlands, 2011, p. 29). The first of these reports simply assumes the category 'Asian-American' refers to Americans of Chinese heritage when in fact the US category is an aggregate of numerous ethnic groups and nationalities (Tamayo-Lott, 1998). It is actually difficult to determine the suicide rate of American woman of Chinese background but, even if it were possible, there is no data to establish causality between suicide and parental expectations. In fact, in the study the reporter is referring to (www.sciencedaily.com/releases/2009/08/090817190650. htm) the lead author declares, 'It is unclear why Asian-Americans who are born in the US have higher rates of thinking about and attempting suicide'. The study, as such, does not actually measure suicide rates. It is also difficult to find accurate suicide figures for China, and those which are available not only vary but, once again, do not indicate causality. While a myriad of factors could contribute to suicide rates among youth both within China and abroad, it is simply convenient to assume high pressure parenting is the cause. Yet, beyond this, using ethnicity as a category of analysis simply foregrounds and sometimes isolates one aspect of social being. It is also a useful mechanism for establishing boundaries, 'we do this' but 'they do that'. While 'no culture is ever a fully consistent or coherent whole' (Parekh, 2002, p. 152), this is a popular conception fed by the media, reproduced within the public consciousness and, once established, it is difficult to shift.

Beyond tiger mothers: An Asian invasion?

Negative reaction to Chinese success is also evident in the Western media's response to the results of different national and international testing programmes. In Australia, reports referring to the academic performance of Chinese (or 'Asian') students begin to appear regularly from the early 2000s. In many ways this increased reportage of Chinese success articulates a new variation on Australia's 'invasion anxiety' stemming from the insecurity arising out of Australia's status as a white, postcolonial Anglo nation in an Asian region (Burke, 2008). Although Chinese migration to Australia dates back to the Gold Rushes of the 1850s, the limits to non-white migration for most of the first half of the twentieth century achieved through the White Australia Policy meant that it was not until the early 1990s that greater numbers of Chinese began to settle in Australia. Following the Tiananmen Square Massacre in 1989, the Australian Prime Minister, Bob Hawke, granted asylum to the 42,000 Chinese students in Australia at that time. Chinese migration has since risen rapidly, as has the media coverage of Chinese students' remarkable academic success. In September 2001, it was acknowledged in the *Brisbane Courier Mail* with the headline 'Improved by Asian Work Ethic'. Here commentator Michael Duffy began his discussion of the phenomenon by indicating he has no 'racist intentions', something he feels obliged to declare given 'those who raise the subject are 'routinely accused of paranoia and holding irrational fears of Australia being "flooded" by aliens' (Duffy, 2001, p. 28). Such remarks not only attest to the public awareness of the success of Asian students by this time but of a racist backlash in response. Although purporting to look at how Asian success can motivate other students to improve their results, Duffy's opinion piece clearly represents the Asian, and primarily Chinese, student as Other, in direct competition with the Anglo majority. He highlights their 'disproportionate numbers' in selective schools and elite university courses and how they 'dominate' lists of top performing students. In trying to account for this success, Duffy considers the possibility that 'Chinese people are smarter' together with reference to the phenomenon of 'migrant drive'. The central cause, however, he sees is 'hard work', yet this is linked to 'widespread' coaching which is framed as a kind of unfair advantage. The increase in coaching colleges is seen to be a direct result of the influx of Chinese and other Asian migrants, despite the long-standing use of private tutors by high SES parents and despite the increasing privatization of educational services generally over the last 20 years. The emphasis throughout the piece is on cultural difference with Duffy concluding that some Chinese see the Australian image as 'irrelevant or as a bloated decaying carcass, with its emphasis on losers, defeat, oppression and victims'. Such comments position the 'over-achieving' Chinese against the 'easy-going' Australian, with the achievement of Chinese students more akin to cultural incursion than indicative of the success of Australian multiculturalism.

Reports on the number of Chinese or Asian students in selective high schools appear regularly in the Australian press. In 2002, for example, in an article titled 'Selected for their strengths – The Cultural Divide' the national broadsheet *The Australian* detailed how large numbers of Asian students in Sydney's selective high schools was causing concern among 'old boys', with a call to alter their selection criteria. Outside coaching was seen to 'skew enrolment' and account for the large number of Asian students (Yaman, 2002, p. 10). Many of those considered Asian were in fact Australian-born. As one parent of Chinese background pointed out, '. . . you can look Chinese, like my daughter [who is] a second generation Australian and be standing next to someone who had just arrived from England. How many generations do you have to be in Australia to be considered Australian?' In 2004, as an indication of the level of anxiety over the ethnic mix of students in selective high schools and primary school Opportunity Classes (OCs) for the 'academically gifted', the entrance exams were changed. Prior to this, the exams tested English, Maths and General Knowledge using multiple choice questions, but a new writing component was added; no doubt in an attempt to counter any perceived advantage Asian students may have had through coaching. Despite criticism by the Chinese-speaking community of an ethnic bias prompted by the changes, the additional test had little impact on the numbers of Asian students gaining entry to selective schools and media reports on this trend continued unabated (*NDT*, 2002, p. 8).

In 2005 *The Sydney Morning Herald* reported on the 'Chinese Revolution Sweeping Our Schools', listing the percentage of LBOTE students in all NSW selective high schools (Doherty, 2005, p. 1). Emphasis was placed on the Chinese with allusions to the threat of invasion; the recurrent trope in accounts of Chinese migration. The number of Chinese students attending these schools, however, is difficult to determine given the lack of disaggregated data. The article refers to Chinese-speaking migrants from Hong-Kong, Singapore, Malaysia and Mainland China, but the category 'Chinese' is favoured with occasional references to 'Asians'. The significance of this article is the way in which it attributes academic performance to ethnic background, as a cultural trait related to a student's Confucian heritage. Confucianism is often used as a shorthand explanation for Chinese success, as if Confucian values of hard work and honouring authority had remained unchanged over centuries and were simply passed down from parent to child, over time and across national boundaries (e.g. Garnaut, 2010, p. 23; Haines, 2011, p. 26).

This supposed Confucian ethic, however, is typically problematized, as Clark and Gieve (2006) show, by equating it with negative attributes. Chinese students are presented as lacking creativity, as 'kinds of automatons' without 'sufficient socialisation experience' (Stevenson and Patty, 2010, p. 11). *The Age* newspaper, for example, drew on the insights of a US-based academic, Professor Yong Zhao, to make a similar point that 'a narrow focus on academic excellence doesn't develop the sort of emotional intelligence required for leadership, creativity, risk-taking, entrepreneurship, the ability to network with others' (Milburn, 2011, p. 15). Concern is also expressed over 'how students who focus on academic brilliance can end up unprepared for the real world' and 'that the same cultural values that emphasize and facilitate educational achievement may also promote silence on the expression of social and psychological needs' (Milburn, 2011, p. 8). One article cites a psychologist who declares, 'My experience is that some Asian children are incredibly stressed' and another quotes a principal who points out that, to apply 'excessive pressure . . . is to deny them a childhood' (Patty, 2008a, p. 9). There are also articles that most overtly pathologize the success of Chinese students such as: 'The China Syndrome: the sum of genes, culture and language', which reports on 'a theory that people of a southern Chinese background have a highly developed work ethic focused on problem solving from thousands of years tending to rice paddies' (Gilmore, 2009, p. 15). While varied, media coverage of Chinese success often presents it as a form of deviant, cultural pathology which seems to directly threaten core social values and to 'take over' Australian society. Rarely are the practices in which students engage considered constitutive of an *academic* culture which are requisite for scholarly endeavour, promoted more so in some families than others irrespective of their ethnic background. With the media fuelling public anxieties over multicultural education, however, it is ethnicity that is foregrounded and it is this which is presented as the key driver of academic success.

Amidst the media coverage of the success of Chinese students, occasional reference is made to the phenomenon of 'white flight', the Anglo avoidance of schools with concentrations of LBOTE students. While the prevalence of such a phenomenon is difficult to determine, there are many schools with low numbers of ESB students and concentrations of those with a LBOTE. While not to discount the influence of racism, this may also relate to the socio-economic background of a school's drawing area together with its settlement history and other factors. One front-page newspaper report in 2008 referred to schools that are perceived as being predominantly 'Lebanese, Muslim and Asian schools' and which Anglo parents tend to avoid (Patty, 2008b, p. 1). Articles on white flight from 'Asian schools', however, seem to be a correlate of those that focus on the large numbers of Chinese students in selective schools, yet with something of a twist. Rather than Anglo students seen as being displaced by higher performing Chinese who gain entry with the assistance of coaching – what one report (Patty, 2009, p. 3) indicated Anglo-Australians saw as 'beneath them or 'a form of cheating' – white flight is presented as a mechanism for avoiding the competition in the first place, presented as a cultural preference for a well-rounded education rather than 'academic hot-housing' (Milburn, 2010, p. 17).

Ho (2011) discusses the phenomenon of white flight in her account of schools as micropublics, sites where cultural difference is negotiated and transcended. She finds government policy in Australia around school choice with the proliferation of government selective schools and the public funding of private schools as working against the way in which schools perform the important role of facilitating intercultural understanding. This is the case given the concentrations of students from various Asian backgrounds in selective schools and the predominance of Anglo students in private schools. Promoting comprehensive schools over those with selective enrolments she sees as one way of ensuring a more even spread of ethnic diversity across school populations. Yet, with ethnicity dominating debates about academic performance, public anxieties over multicultural education continue to fester, skewing perceptions about educational achievement and the role of schooling.

Media representation of Pasifika students

While Chinese students are perceived as high achievers, those of Pasifika backgrounds are associated with the other end of the spectrum. Typically, media representation of Pasifika students focuses on the negative. In Australia, though, media attention is given to the involvement of Pasifika youth in crime and gang-related violence rather than their educational performance per se. Headlines such as 'Police tackle Islander Gangs' (Bartock, 2009), 'Pacific Islanders Contribute to Sydney Gang Problem' (Morri, 2011), 'Pacifika Program Endeavours to Keep Kids out of Jail' (O'Neill, 2009), 'Pacific Islander Elders in Bid to Stop Crime on Streets' (Robinson, 2010) exemplify this trend. Brief references are made to poor educational performance, underlining the link between social marginalization and educational 'failure' and the fears of a growing underclass among Australia's Pacific Islander population (AAP, 2002; Hildebrand, 2003; Fynes-Clinton, 2011). Alternatively, there is slightly more positive media representation of Pasifika youths' involvement in sport, especially in the different rugby codes where they have a strong presence. Even here, though, stories may be given a negative slant with Pasifika youth seen to have an unfair size and weight advantage over Anglo-Australians. One article reporting on the impact of Pasifika players in junior leagues portrays this as a potential danger with 'non-Islander parents pulling their sons out of both codes (union and league) because of concerns for their safety' (Lane, 2006). Perhaps there is little mention of Pasifika youth in relation to education as, unlike the Chinese, they are not seen as a threat to the Anglo majority, at least not in terms of academic achievement. Rather, threats are couched more in terms of a troubling physical presence on the sports field and on the streets where the threat to the Anglo 'mainstream' is more explicit.

While little attention is given to the educational achievement of Pasifika students in the Australian press, in New Zealand, with a far larger population of migrants from various Pacific Islander communities together with the Indigenous Māori, the situation is quite different. Regular reports on the academic performance of Māori and Pacific Islanders appear in the New Zealand press, though coverage, once again, is generally negative. Very often Māori and Pacific Islander students are compared to those of Asian and Pakeha (Anglo) backgrounds. The *Dominion Post* from Wellington, for example, reports that 'the gulf between our best and worst pupils is wide by international standards and Maori and Pacific Islander pupils continue to perform worse than Pakeha and Asian children' (Nichols, 2006, p. 8). Another report refers to how 'Poor university entrance results among Pacific Islander pupils have prompted calls for a national strategy to address under performance'. It points out how results show that '73.7% of Asian pupils who make up the highest-performing ethnic group achieved university entrance . . . the rate for Pacific Islander pupils, however, is less than half, at 36.4%' (Fisher, 2011, p. 10). Another presents similar findings that, 'from a roll of 41,000, Auckland University has 14,600 Asian students' and, while the report couldn't provide a further breakdown, it indicated 'Chinese are thought to outnumber Pacific Islanders (3210) and Maori (2789) combined' (Cumming, 2011, www.nzherald.co.nz/nz/news/article.cfm?c_id=1&objectid=10718642). Another report even quotes a New Zealand academic declaring that 'If only Pakeha and Asian students went to school in New Zealand, we'd perform at the top of the world. If only Māori and Pacific Islander went to school in New Zealand, then Turkey is the only country that [would] perform worse' (Collins, 2010, www.nzherald.co.nz/nz/news/article.cfm?c_id=1&objectid=10747700).

These articles are indicative of the way in which performance data is reported, cementing ideas about the relation between ethnicity, social disadvantage and academic achievement, prompting ethnically framed institutional responses that simply reinforce such trends. Recognition of cultural identity through the use of culturally inclusive curricula is often considered a way of lifting the performance of students from particular ethnic backgrounds that may be underperforming. The *Dominion Post* reports how Dr Leone Pihama, a leading Māori academic, is of the view 'that if positive changes are to occur for Maori . . . the curriculum needs to better reflect Maori cultural identity, and Maori pupils have to arrive at school feeling good about themselves' (Nichols, 2006, p. 8). While education systems have an ethical obligation to use culturally inclusive curricula and, as Dr Pihama indicates, it may have certain psychological pay-offs such as an increased motivation to learn, achievement is not simply a function of psychological well-being. It is dependent upon the capacities students have embodied; habits of learning acquired through iterative practice that in themselves can provide the motor to achieve.

Culturally inclusive curricula may also have its drawbacks. While intending to be representative of various ethnic groups, it can lapse into a kind of *well-meaning essentialism*, presenting reductive cultural stereotypes that students, with more hybrid identities, are more likely to reject given they poorly reflect their actual experience of everyday life. Either way, such measures do not directly address the issue of improving academic performance given ethnicity, rather than the capacities that promote learning, is the focus. Instead, ethnicity becomes 'the problem' as is evident in another New Zealand article headlined, 'Polynesians lag behind at school'. Reporting on a 2001–2005 overview of student outcomes, it claims 'Maori and Pacific Islander pupils are handicapped by starting school with lower comprehension skills'. It points out that 'While the two ethnicities can learn at the same rate as other pupils, they start school with a big disadvantage, including their knowledge of books and the alphabet' (Nichols and Bennetts, 2006, p. 6). Here, the lack of skills is linked to ethnicity as if one determined the other. Rather than the students themselves given agency to learn, the 'two ethnicities' have been assigned this role colouring perceptions of student performance even prior to school. Limited alphabetic knowledge and minimal familiarity with books, however, is more likely a result of socio-economic factors and the specific practices students engage in than a function of ethnicity. The pre-literacy skills of many low SES Anglo students are also often quite poor yet ethnicity is never considered a factor in explaining their poor performance. As Ahmed (2004, p. 2) points out, drawing on the work of Londe, 'the production of whiteness works precisely by assigning race to others'. Being Anglo or white operates as a neutral category devoid of any ethno-racial markers. In relation to non-whites, however, this aspect of identification is foregrounded and, as in this news report, obscures more probable explanations for the limited literacy skills of these children. Another article in the *Dominion Post* addresses this more directly. It quotes the Pasifika Assistant Vice-Chancellor of Victoria University who refers to the impact of immigration and socio-economic factors as affecting the academic performance of Pasifika students. She calls for homework centres to be established to provide additional support for students given many have parents who are unable to supervise their children's work (Fisher, 2011, p. 10).

More often than not, though, blame is levelled at ethnicity, race or culture, which are seen as synonyms. A letter to this effect in *The New Zealand Herald* laments the way in which the nation is handicapped by its cultural diversity. It claims that it is 'largely monocultural countries like Denmark and Korea' that perform better in international testing programmes but that 'New Zealand has always had two cultures at least and latterly a whole bunch more'.[3] Māori and Pacific Islander students are singled out as 'tailenders in the New Zealand education system' (Anonymous, 2008, p. 11). The letter effectively absolves the nation from blame depicting it as a victim of the heterogeneous mix of its own population; happy it seems to claim Pakeha success but keen to excise the failure it attributes to 'the rest'. Fault is not only given to 'cultures' here in an abstract sense as reified blocs of the population, somehow sectioned-off as distinct groups. The letter also targets parents of particular cultural backgrounds positioning them as Other and assigning them responsibility for the nation's uneven performance declaring, 'It is all too easy to blame "the system" or schools or teachers . . . but the real fault lies elsewhere – with the parents.' In contrast to the Chinese, Pacific Islander parents are portrayed as far too lax and uninterested in their children's education, attitudes that are then presented as cultural traits common to entire communities.

Even good news stories about Pasifika students seem to be given a negative slant in the New Zealand press. A 2007 article in *The New Zealand Herald*, reporting on increased numbers of Pacific Islander students in early childhood education, completing high school, obtaining apprenticeships and entering tertiary education, chose to focus on negative data given less prominence in the article featuring the headline 'Pacific Island suspension rate up 20 pc in six years' (McKenzie-Minifie, 2007, p. 9). Similarly, another report in *The New Zealand Herald* in 2010 chose the headline, 'Too many Pasifika students falling through the cracks, says report', when the article demonstrates improved performance, including a 53 per cent increase over 5 years in the number of Pasifika students completing the final year of school. The 'falling through the cracks' actually refers to how the report featured in the article indicates the ways in which teachers often provide poor career advice to Pasifika students and only contact the parents 'when something bad has happened' (Collins, 2010, p. 2). Rather than singling out schools, teachers and current practices for criticism, the headline casts the students as victims, implying failure on their part. It simply reproduces the same old perceptions about the academic performance of Pasifika students and the supposed impact of ethnicity on educational achievement. It also demonstrates a similar anxiety around multicultural education that exists elsewhere in other Western migrant nations; the ways in which the Other either 'shows up' or 'brings down' the Anglo majority.

Ethnicity, categories and group coherence

While education is not seen as a priority for Pasifika families in the same way it is for the Chinese, what is common to both is the same essentializing of their ethnicity and the way in which this is used as a rationale for their academic performance. This is not only evident in the media, studies of educational achievement regularly use ethnicity as a category of analysis conflating notions of category and group as if they were one and the same thing (Brubaker, 2004). Categories used to signify ethnicity, such as 'Chinese' or 'Pacific Islander', need not necessarily signify 'groupness' in the sense of being a part of a coherent whole. Such labels are merely one form of identification that needs to be understood as inherently variable denoting difference along with sameness. This is made plain with a category like 'Anglo' which has a far less defined groupness, if any at all. Categories of non-Anglo ethnicity operate quite differently. They seem to possess a certain 'stickiness' wherein particular traits are assumed to be indicative of all those assigned that ethnicity (Ahmed, 2004). This is true even with a category like 'Pasifika' which includes a diverse range of peoples.

As Brubaker (2004, p. 12) argues, 'By distinguishing consistently between categories and groups, we can problematize – rather than presume – the relation between them'. If not, we can fall into the trap of using a category like 'ethnicity' as an explanation in itself. This is not only evident in the media; it also frames much educational research around academic achievement. In their US-based study, Pang et al. (2011, p. 384), for example, declare 'that ethnicity continues to be the main effect when comparing White Americans, Chinese Americans and Samoan Americans in reading and math'. Their study is significant in that it problematizes the macro-category of 'Asian American Pacific Islander' (AAPI) often used in US population data and much social research, claiming that it masks the great diversity of 'cultures and communities' it represents. Pang et al. challenge the view of AAPI students as a 'model minority' of high achievers by disaggregating achievement data into 13 AAPI sub-groups to demonstrate the variable internal achievement of, for example, White, Chinese and Samoan Americans. Pang et al. do not only focus on the academic achievement of more refined categories of ethno-racial membership within the larger category of AAPI, they also give consideration to gender and socio-economic background, together with explaining how other factors such as language and the lack of culturally relevant curriculum may impact upon student performance. Despite this, and the undeniable importance of demonstrating the uselessness of a category like AAPI, the ethno-racial categories they retain in their analysis unproblematically equate category with group even it seems in the case of 'White American'. While the varied nature of the academic performance of the AAPI sub-groups is acknowledged, variation internal to these is not. Ethnicity, therefore, is still presented as a major determinant of academic achievement when in fact a child's individual performance may result from an array of factors. Pang et al. seem to acknowledge this but have difficulty viewing categories of race, ethnicity and culture in fluid terms, possessing 'blurred boundaries' that 'flow, change, intermingle, cut across and through one another' (Holliday et al., 2004, p. 4). Instead, they are treated as things, becoming objects of analysis with a discursive authority that is difficult to counter, particularly given their reproduction in the media. Such categories become the lens through which academic performance is perceived framing public perceptions of student achievement and inflaming anxieties over the impact of cultural diversity on education.

Concluding remarks

This chapter has explored what we have called the ethnicization of educational achievement drawing on the media portrayal of 'Chinese success' and the social marginalization of Pasifika students. Where a more conventional analysis of the relationship between ethnicity and education might have summarized the vast literature on educational outcomes analysed in terms of categories of ethnic or cultural background, we have started somewhere else, with a different aim. We wish to problematize the very categories that are used, both academically and in popular debate, to make sense of the differential performances of students from diverse backgrounds.

Too easily in popular debates categories of ethnicity become the explanation of social phenomena, not a means by which those complexities can be unpacked. The media have a crucial role to play in shaping public perceptions of the educational achievement of LBOTE students and encourages the view that ethnicity has a determining role. This is of course not unique to the media. Much academic literature serves to reinforce this perspective, using categories of ethnicity as distinct markers of group membership and so simplifying analysis. Yet, as Wicker (1997, p. 360) points out, 'We need to accept that cultures and ethnic groups as actual autonomous totalities do not exist – or, at least, no longer exist'. There are, of course, quite deep investments in the ways we think about ethnicity and culture – we have pointed to the ways in which debates about Tiger Mothers, for example, rest on broader social anxieties – and so we have spent some time trying to draw out the problems with these social perceptions.

We take this line not because we think ethnicity and culture are irrelevant, but because the ways these categories are perceived as groups with fixed and everlasting boundaries, reified attributes and cultural pathologies gets in the way of understanding complex social, cultural and educational processes. We would argue that ethnicity is best understood as forms of identification which are constructed through diverse forms of practice and relationship, and while this view of ethnicity is not the main focus on the book, an emphasis on practice is central to the book's argument. From the discussion of Tiger Mothers and Pasifika students we want to pursue three particular lines of enquiry which we think provide insight into the relationship between ethnicity and education. First, we wish to shift the focus to the role of social practices as fundamental to the production of educational capacities and their uneven distribution. To do this, we start with the *dispositions* to schooling that students exhibit and we use these not to categorize students by ethnicity, but to think about the practices which produce those capacities. Second, we want to explore the pedagogies of school and home, and the ways that these different domains foster the particular kinds of practices that contribute to the formation of particular dispositions, some more and some less conducive to academic engagement. Third, extending our arguments about the social perceptions of ethnicity in media representations and academic research, we suggest that teachers themselves adopt particular ethnicized schemas of perception of students and their parents which participate in the distribution of academic outcomes. These arguments have critical consequences both for classroom practices and the home–school relationship – indeed, they pose particular challenges to the ways we understand multicultural education.

2

Surveying culture and educational capital

So far we have argued that discussions of the relationship between culture and education draw too heavily on problematic perceptions of ethnicity. This is not to say that use of such categories to make sense of educational data is entirely useless. Indeed, broad statistical analyses provide a useful starting point for making sense of the complex relationship between ethnic background and educational performance. Yet, as we spell out in the Introduction, despite persistent assumptions of 'ethnic disadvantage' and 'ethnic drive', the data show that there is no universal factor of ethnicity related to achievement – rather, there are substantial differences on the broader bases of SES, demonstrating the complexity of the relationships between ethnicity, language, SES, gender and between the first, second and third generations, and between complex histories of migration (Kalantzis and Cope, 1988; Khoo and Birrell, 2002; Matthews, 2002; Lew, 2006; Shah et al., 2010). A relatively recent review of the data in the United Kingdom, for example, has suggested that the performance of students from ethnic minorities is shaped by a complex of factors, grouped in terms of structural features (e.g. social class), dynamic aspects of family context (e.g. parental aspirations), pupil characteristics (e.g. motivation) and school context or type (Strand, 2007, p. 7).

Despite the criticisms, there is some patterning in the links between ethnicity and educational achievement, at least for some groups. The occupational and educational success of Chinese migrants in the West has been extensively documented (Francis and Archer, 2005; Costigan et al., 2010; Pang et al., 2011). Chinese background students in Australia, for example, are more likely to complete Year 12, achieve better results, gain a University degree and be in managerial or professional employment than most other groups (Jones, 2005). In contrast, a large body of research, especially in New Zealand, illustrates the poor educational performance of Pasifika students

(Nash, 2000; Flockton and Crooks, 2001, 2003; Horsley and Walker, 2004; Valdez et al., 2007). As we have suggested in the Introduction, this cannot be explained by a simplistic assertion of deeply shared cultural values but entails a range of factors which are realized in and through familial and institutional contexts (Francis and Archer, 2005).

The creation of family environments in which there are strong demands for educational achievement, values of effort, restraint and industry (Rosenthal and Feldman, 1991), then, is less to do with overarching, ethnically defined values than a combination of factors. Moreover, these elements have to connect with the institutional practices of the educational system. Campbell and Verna (2007) argue that the formation of 'academic home climates' is central to the success of gifted children, especially when they mesh with the academic climate found in the school. Recent research into the success of Chinese background students in mathematics suggests that whatever success is achieved is due to a combination of good teaching and motivation to achieve, parental help and extra study (Cao et al., 2006; Zhao et al., 2006; Zhao and Singh, 2011) a finding echoed in earlier work (McInerney and McInerney, 1994).

This research suggests that a more thorough-going analysis of educational performance would move from broad aggregations of data to analyses of practice, both in schools and homes, which aid participation in schooling, and to see these in terms of patterns of ethnicity; not to confirm cultural pathologies but to open up our analysis of complex practices. Drawing on the practice-based approach of Bourdieu and his conceptualization of cultural capital, we will use the idea of educational capital to provide a broad brushstrokes picture of the students and their parents in this chapter, and then offer a more nuanced approach in the next. This chapter presents data derived from the survey of parents of Year 3 students in ten schools across Sydney. As we have outlined, the objective of the survey was to collect information on the different ethnic groups within each school that was relevant to the wider research questions as well as to inform later phases of the research. Responses to the survey questions allowed us to develop some initial insights into the relationships between parents' ethnicity, their educational capital and home practices, students' experiences at school and their dispositions to learning addressed in detail later in the book.

Culture and capitals

Bourdieu (1986) develops his notion of cultural capital – as the learned competence in the valued ways of doing things – as a way of explaining the unequal educational performance of students. It sits alongside economic capital and social capital (or the networks of social connection) as key forms through which class relations of power are reproduced. After the primary role of the family, he argues that schools have a secondary but fundamental role in the reproduction of cultural capital as a way of legitimising the values and beliefs of the dominant class. For Bourdieu (1986), cultural capital takes three forms: as *embodied* dispositions of mind and body; in an *objectified* state (e.g. books, artworks), and *institutionalized* through educational qualifications. Initially, Bourdieu saw this in terms of the reproduction of power, and argued that these forms of competence serve merely to 'consecrate' the 'cultural arbitrary' of class-based knowledge and values (Bourdieu and Passeron, 1990). Bourdieu, (1984, p. 23), for example, talks about 'academic capital', as a form of cultural capital, as:

> the guaranteed product of the combined effects of cultural transmission by the family and cultural transmission by the school (the efficiency of which depends on the amount of cultural capital directly inherited from the family). Through its value-inculcating and value-imposing operations, the school also helps (to a greater or lesser extent, depending on the initial disposition, i.e., class of origin) to form a general, transposable disposition towards legitimate culture, which is first acquired with respect to scholastically recognized knowledge and practices but tends to be applied beyond the bounds of the curriculum, taking the form of a 'disinterested' propensity to accumulate experience and knowledge which may not be directly profitable in the academic market.

Alongside class, Bourdieu's framework has been taken up by scholars exploring questions of gender and ethnicity as forms of social inequality (Reay, 1998; Modood, 2004). Yet as fruitful as this framework has proved, especially through its linking of home and school, it reduces all educational knowledge and skills, including literacy and numeracy, to a social mechanism of distinction and the legitimation and reproduction of social power. Bourdieu (1996) later acknowledged that cultural competences such as reading are also functional or 'technical', in that they have a basis in performing certain tasks and are not just mechanisms that distribute people into positions of power. Much as Wall et al. (1998) have done in unpacking different takes on social capital as a resource, a goal-orientation (to enhance one's status) and as a mechanism of social control, we think that there needs to be a shift back towards examining the 'productive', resourceful dimension of cultural capital, not as a way of avoiding the question of power – indeed, we believe it is necessary to better understand its reproductive dimension in relation to social relations – but as a way of fleshing out the diverse dimensions of cultural capital relevant to education. Not all educational knowledge is the class-based knowledge of the powerful, but includes socially useful skills that are largely monopolized by the powerful.

Central here is the role of the home. Bourdieu suggests that the fundamental relation between family, class and education is much more complicated than we normally imagine, but he rarely explores this in all its complexity and in particular says little about ethnicity. While Bourdieu's conception of forms of capital is more productive than those sociologists of education who have perceived 'family background' as primarily a reflection of larger class structures which determine educational attainment (Bowles and Gintis, 1976), he has not written, as Reay (1998) argues, directly on home-school relationships, nor on the socialized capacities that enable educational participation.

To begin to explore these issues, we use the term 'educational capital' to cover an array of competencies, skills and knowledges (Howard et al., 1996; Fay, 2001). These competencies range from an understanding of the schooling system (a significant form of knowledge for many from migrant or poor backgrounds) to foundational capacities such as writing to higher order forms of knowledge. Such competencies are distributed unevenly, according to SES, ethnicity, gender and so on, but they are not reducible to these broad social categories nor to the reproduction of systems of power. A more cautious analysis of educational performance, we would argue, would demonstrate the ways these competencies exist in relationship to the formation of students' habitus and dispositions towards learning.[1]

Although educational capital is 'possessed' by an individual or a family, it is also a question of how this synchronizes with the values and practices of the educational system which shapes educational participation. Marjoribanks (1979, 2002) has attempted to elaborate the multiple dimensions of these relationships. In particular, he examines the nexus between ethnicity and class through an unpacking of various dimensions of family background, structure, values and orientations to achievement, and how these relate to educational capital, school structures and student characteristics, recognizing that each element mediates and moderates the effects of the others. In the educational and psychological literature there is a wealth of research into various aspects of the role of the family environment and 'effective parenting'. Campbell and Verna (2007), for example, draw together much of this research and formulate a notion of a positive 'academic home climate' which promotes curiosity and encourages the child to pursue their academic interests. This generates positive behaviours, attitudes, beliefs and values that lead to children having higher levels of achievement. This is especially true, they argue, when the academic home climate is in sync with the school's academic climate. Yet the level of theorization which ties these insights together – as educational capital – is often missing.

Reay (1998, pp. 57–9) outlines a number of aspects of cultural capital relevant to schooling that would constitute educational capital: material resources, educational qualifications, available time, information about the educational system, social confidence, educational knowledge and the ease with which parents approach teaching staff. Lee and Bowen (2006) argue educational capital exists in three forms: personal dispositions, attitudes and knowledge; connections to education-related objects, books, computers, and connections to education-related institutions, for example, universities, libraries. At stake here is the effort parents invest in their children's education. Like Reay, Lareau (2011), in her research among families from different socio-economic backgrounds, argues that middle class parents tend to adopt a strategy she calls 'concerted cultivation' which entails high levels of parental intervention in their children's after-school lives that prepares them for professional futures. Working-class and parents from low socio-economic backgrounds, by contrast, tend to invest much less effort in organizing their children's lives and directing them towards educational success. Outcomes, then, are seen more as the 'accomplishment of natural growth'. The consequence of this, however, is that working class child-rearing is out of sync with the standards of the educational institution (Lareau, 2011, p. 3). The educational capital developed within the middle-class home is more closely aligned with the dominant set of cultural repertoires that comprise the standards and policies of institutions like the school and work. This research suggests a close relationship between the spheres of the home and the school, and the spheres of the parent and the child, which in turn mirrors the expectations of the teacher and school. Unfortunately much of the research focuses on class and has much less to say about race and ethnicity, or when it does discuss these aspects, it tends to deemphasize them in relation to class (Lareau, 2011). For parents from culturally and linguistically diverse backgrounds it is not simply class that shapes these practices, but divergent experiences relating to migration and cultural difference. Home and school environments differ considerably and so do parents from different cultural, linguistic and socio-economic backgrounds differ in their type of involvement in supporting their children's learning. Variations in parent involvement may derive from differences in educational knowledge, cultural practices and financial resources. Educational capital deriving from family background becomes increasingly significant when we factor in the increasing emphasis placed on parental involvement in school over the last few decades (Henderson and Berla, 1995; Cuttance and Stokes, 2000; Barnard, 2004; Sheldon and Epstein, 2005; Epstein et al., 2009), because not all parents are equally at home in the cultures of schooling and their unequal resources inhibit the capacity of parents to perform any of these roles effectively.

Our survey attempted to capture something of these aspects of educational capital: parents' backgrounds, engagement with school, values around learning at home, extracurricular activities and parents' perceptions of their child's educational achievement as a framing devise for analysing students' capacities in more nuanced ways. The survey reveals some very broad patterns around the connections between SES and educational orientation, and significant differences between the three groups under examination.

The survey sample

The survey was distributed to an initial group of ten schools with three schools from Group 1, three from Group 2 and four from Group 3. Four schools were included in Group 3 due to the difficulties involved in finding schools with a significant representation of both Chinese and Pasifika students. This additional school was surveyed to allow for greater choice in the selection process for interviews and observations. In all, a total of 469 parents were surveyed, representing a range of language groups and countries of birth. Within this larger sample, 311 parents across the three ethnic groups targeted here returned the survey. The number of surveys returned from each of the ethnic groups targeted varied considerably: 154 were of Chinese background, 38 of Pasifika background and 119 of Anglo background. Based on the representation of these groups across the surveyed schools, this indicates a return rate from Chinese parents approximately double that of Anglo and Pasifika parents. This may suggest that among Chinese parents there is a greater investment in education, educational research and a familiarity with schooling, and an expectation of possible benefits for their children – evidence of educational capital.

This survey tried to document some key aspects of the forms of educational capital held by parents. The findings proved interesting in relation to the differences between ethnic groups but are not presented here in terms of a detailed statistical analysis, especially given that there were no equivalent samples of each group. Instead, the focus is on identifying broad trends and establishing a broad context for understanding each of the schools and groups. Given the established links between social class and educational attainment, we provide some information related to SES (income, occupation and qualifications), before we explore parents' participation in school, academic engagement at home, extracurricular activities and views of their child's academic achievements. These provide a broad context to later arguments, drawing on interview and observational data, about the different patterns of educational orientation among the three groups.

The backgrounds of parents

Questions related to parents' own experiences and influencing factors helped to develop a profile of the respondents and establish a notion of cultural identity beyond simple ethnicity. One such issue was the respondents' own education which is significant not only in terms of each group's aspirations for their own children's education but what it suggests about the parent's educational capital and the process of educational reproduction. Many studies examine the correlations between parents' income, level of education and their children's educational achievement (Bowles and Gintis, 1976; Sticht, 1988; Haveman and Wolfe, 1996; Mortimore, 1997; Anderson and Bruce, 2004; Teese, 2007). In this study, a similar, broad correlation was evident. Chinese and Anglo parents had the highest levels of education, with 74 per cent of Chinese and 60 per cent of Anglo respondents having completed post-secondary educational qualifications, compared to just 23 per cent of those of Pasifika background. Anglo parents also had the highest proportion of higher degree qualifications, whereas none of the Pasifika respondents had tertiary qualifications. This suggests that our Chinese and Anglo samples tended to be better qualified than the respective ethnic categories nationally: in the 2001 census only 40 per cent of those of Chinese ancestry and 36 per cent of those of English-speaking heritage had a post-school qualification, while our Pasifika sample was relatively comparable with the national figures, with 27 per cent having a post-school qualification (ABS, 2007).

As with the parents' educational qualifications, figures on income also revealed differences between the three groups. The survey revealed that Anglo respondents were the highest income-earners, with 56 per cent earning above $60,000, compared to just 13 per cent of the Pasifika respondents. In comparison, 56 per cent of Pasifika parents earned less than $A40,000. The income bracket representation of Chinese respondents varied significantly, with the same percentage of Chinese parents earning less than $A20,000 as those earning above $A80,000. While the Anglo sample in the project was, however, faring better than the national figures for this group (only 37% earn more than $A60,000), the Chinese and Pasifika samples tended to be doing less well than their group nationally (ABS, 2007).[2]

A similar pattern can be seen in relation to occupations. Anglo parents were more likely to have a professional or managerial position (33%) than either Chinese parents (21%) or Pasifika parents (8%). Anglos were also less likely to be unemployed or work in manual labour (1%) compared to Chinese (12%) and Pasifika (21%). Again, this means our Anglo sample is somewhat better off than the nationwide group, although the comparisons for Chinese and Pasifika groups are more complex. Only 23 per cent of Anglo adults are in professional or managerial positions nationally, and 5 per cent in manual employment, while the unemployment rate is 4.6 per cent. The corresponding figures for the Chinese are 24, 4.7 and 5.6 per cent, while for Pasifika adults they are 11, 12 and 9 per cent.

These distributions are largely reflections of the SES of the suburban locations of the schools. Income and occupation are often taken as the simplest measure of social class, and then correlated with educational outcomes (Bowles and Gintis, 1976), yet, as we have suggested, large analytical categories such as *class* (like *ethnicity*) are useful only up to a point. As they operate at a macro level, they provide little insight, for example, into how economically advantaged children actually acquire the competencies that are inequitably distributed. Many key approaches to social reproduction, such as those of Bourdieu and of Bowles and Gintis, are concerned with the ways schooling legitimizes the cultural capital of the privileged, not how they *acquire* that capital. They also operate on the assumption that dominant forms of knowledge are simply mechanisms of class control, not socially powerful capacities which are monopolized by the powerful. And they operate with rigid notions of social power, and rarely address the protean nature of class, gender and ethnicity (Collins, 2009). While the socio-economic figures listed above may indicate something of the material resources and qualifications Reay includes in her breakdown of educational capital, they tell us less about how these relate to educational orientations per se. A focus on practices and values can provide a more nuanced analysis yielding interesting insights about differential achievement rates and the complex sociocultural realities behind them. For this reason survey respondents were also asked to provide information about various activities within the home that could impact on their child's educational performance. As mentioned, the nature of the educational capital of parents and children will be developed in later chapters, but it is important here to report some general trends that set the context for these more detailed findings arising from the interviews and observations.

Academic engagement at home

The focus of this part of the survey was on trying to ascertain the ways habits and attitudes of students and parents outside the classroom impact on students' academic performance, and so address issues to do with aspirations, knowledge and orientations to learning established through home practices. As we have earlier indicated, existing research has suggested that achievement motivation, parental help, diligence, independent study and extended application (McInerney et al., 1998; Zhao et al., 2006) are conducive to better educational outcomes. Such attributes and practices are crucial to the knowledges and skills that constitute educational capital through the fostering of a positive 'academic home climate' (Campbell and Verna, 2007). Survey responses reveal differences in the way target group students and parents foster educational capital in the home, around attitudes and practices of academic engagement which instil the valorization of academic pursuits, addressed in the areas of homework practices, extracurricular tasks and reading.

As a starting point, we asked about the amount of homework students undertook. Debates about the usefulness of homework have been around for a long time. This section is not concerned with this, often narrowly framed debate, but with the practices and values adopted by parents of particular groups of students and the ways, as we will develop later in this book, they may relate to the formation of the scholarly habitus. As Laitsch (2006), Xu and Corno (2003) and Dandy and Nettlebeck (2002) note, the value of homework practices, and especially the role of parental assistance, may be less in terms of immediate educational outcomes than in the development of forms of self-discipline, independence, study skills and the creation of an environment conducive to study.

Of the Chinese respondents, 56 per cent stated that their children spent more than one hour on homework each night, compared to 24 per cent of Anglo respondents and 35 per cent for Pasifika parents. The majority of Anglo and Pasifika respondents stated that their child spent 30 minutes on homework per night. The interviews showed that many Chinese students were also doing homework from coaching colleges which could contribute to the extra time spent on homework by this group. The point here is not simply that more homework produces better educational outcomes in and of itself, but that this extra homework demonstrates an extended application to study and the formation of a disciplined approach to academic engagement. In one significant discriminator, 57 per cent of Chinese parents said their child enjoys homework, while only 26 per cent of Anglo parents said they did. The figure for the Pasifika parents – of 87 per cent – wasn't reflected in the interviews, and suggests an example of a tendency among some Pasifika parents to say what they think the interviewers wished to hear. This also links to the point Nash (2000, p. 76) makes that there is a clear gap between the unrealistic aspirations of Pasifika parents and their child's scholastic achievement.

In relation to the supervision of their children's homework, 79 per cent of Anglo, 66 per cent of Chinese and 83 per cent of Pasifika respondents claimed they 'mostly' or 'always' supervise their children's homework. These results tend to suggest an idealized representation of parental help which, again, isn't really borne out by the interview data, particularly in relation to the Pasifika parents. But it is important to record here that this is what the parents have *claimed*. Certainly research has suggested that effective parental help in homework is linked to educational attainment and orientation to schooling (Hoover-Dempsey et al., 2001, 2005). This is linked to the wider point about the significance of direct 'parental effort' in the learning practices of the home – reading, discussions around school, advice, as well as homework itself – in enhancing student outcomes (Barnard, 2004; Houtenville and Conway, 2008; Lareau, 2011).

Xu and Corno (1998) also point to the importance of the creation of an appropriate environment for completing homework, and the role of parents in shaping this and helping their children manage it. The location of the space given over to homework is important because it indicates in the first instance the material resources given over to this activity and the kind of environment in which the children are expected to undertake this work. Of the Chinese respondents, 40 per cent stated that their children do their homework either in their bedroom or in a study, compared to just 13 per cent of Anglo and 25 per cent of Pasifika respondents. Anglo students tended to favour the kitchen or dining room with 69 per cent completing their homework in this area of the home. A similar result of 64 per cent was recorded for Pasifika students. These figures might also suggest something of the different academic focus in the homes of respondents, in particular how Chinese students tend to complete their homework in a space where they may be more inclined to work quietly and independently, removed from areas within the home of greater noise and activity such as kitchens and dining rooms; a point explored in more detail in Chapter 4. These choices will be partly shaped by the family's socio-economic status, of course, but they are not simply reducible to this. Interestingly, Pasifika children were far more likely to do their homework in front of the television ('always', 'mostly' and 'sometimes'), according to their parents (66%) compared to Chinese (42%) and Anglo (31%) students.

Of the Chinese respondents, 95 per cent stated that they give their children extra academic tasks above their normal homework, compared with 57 per cent of Anglo parents. About 92 per cent of Pasifika parents also said they set extra tasks, but this wasn't confirmed in the interview data. Perhaps even more telling was the figure of 21 per cent of Chinese parents who always set extra tasks, compared to 13 per cent for Pasifika parents and 7 per cent of Anglos. Extra academic tasks in this case could be work set by coaching colleges or study guide books purchased from book stores as well as tasks devised by the parents themselves. The importance of this extra work lies not necessarily in its immediate educational benefit, but the extent to which this greater amount supplied by the Chinese parents indicates once again a greater focus on academic engagement within the home. Yet it also has implications for school-based homework, the amounts given and perceived appropriateness.

Of the Anglo respondents, 56 per cent stated that they 'often' read to their children at home, compared to just 18 per cent of Pasifika and 29 per cent of Chinese. These results could be due to both language and time constraints, as well as parental and students' own preferences for independent reading. Either way, much educational research demonstrates the importance of parent reading on early mastery of children's reading (Bus et al., 1995; Myrberg and Rosen, 2009). As Lareau (1989) argues, many (especially middle class) parents invest time and effort in trying to ensure their children gain an 'advantage' through fostering reading competence, and this is crucial to the reproduction of their cultural capital.

The relationship between extracurricular activity and educational attainment is complex and largely under-researched. Much evidence exists which suggests that certain forms of participation in structured activity such as music and sport may correlate with higher academic performance and aspirations (Holland and Andre, 1987; Kluth et al., 2003; Trudeau and Shephard, 2008). Questions regarding extracurricular activities were also included in the survey to establish the way time outside of school was spent and whether trends related to particular activities could be identified. The main activities which respondents nominated as the extracurricular pursuits of their children were music, sport and extra tuition, especially through coaching colleges.

The results for extracurricular music were quite dramatic, with 58 per cent of Chinese respondents stating that their child attended music lessons one or more days per week. This compared with 27 per cent of Anglo respondents' children and just 3 per cent of Pasifika respondents. Interview data revealed that many Pasifika children did attend music activities at settings such as church but these were not considered to be formal 'music lessons' by their parents responding to the survey. Of the Chinese respondents, 33 per cent stated that their children practice more than three days a week. This reveals a significant level of applied discipline and concentration outside the classroom and on a regular basis. This investment of time and money may also be seen to reflect the importance that many Chinese respondents place on this particular activity, either in its own right or as an educationally useful activity. This is of particular interest given that the SES of Chinese respondents varied greatly, but the uptake of extracurricular music seemed to be relatively consistent across SES. The Chinese communities seemed to put a strong emphasis on the development of musicianship and its perceived link to academic ability and discipline. This is different to Scherger and Savage's (2010) discussion of the effect of parental class on educational attainment through the transmission of 'elite' forms of cultural capital via attendance at musical performances (and museums and galleries), but they are not unrelated. However, de Graaf et al. (2000) show that parents' reading behaviour contributes more to a student's educational attainment than 'beaux arts participation'.

As with extracurricular activities generally, the relation between participation in sport and academic success can be ambiguous, although Fejgin (1994) claims a clear and positive correlation for some groups (Sibley and Etnier, 2003; Taras, 2005). Of the Anglo respondents in our sample, 65 per cent stated that their child was involved in an extracurricular sporting activity one or more days a week, with 31 per cent of these attending such activities more than twice a week. In comparison to this, 45 per cent of Chinese children attended sport once a week and 7 per cent more than twice per week. Only 34 per cent of Pasifika students were involved in extracurricular sport: they may have been the most actively involved in sporting activities in the playground and at home, but this didn't seem to translate into involvement in organized sport.

Although Pasifika respondents were not as involved in other areas of extracurricular activities, a significant 48 per cent attended church one or more days a week. This is compared to just 8 per cent of Anglo respondents and 18 per cent of Chinese. This shows that for Pasifika respondents, church and church-related activities occupied a significant proportion of available free time on weekends and during the week. While this attendance may be an important social activity, as well as a religious one, there did not appear to be a transference of skills learned from church-based activities to the educational domain of school and so it didn't accrue the kinds of educational spin-offs that we might associate with other forms of extracurricular activity.

The rise of academic coaching colleges outside school has been one of the most hotly debated features of modern schooling, especially given that they have been linked with students of Asian backgrounds and are perceived to be 'hothouses' which force students to work excessively long hours and foster a toxic competitiveness.[3] Of the Chinese respondents, 39 per cent said that their children attended extracurricular academic coaching one or more days a week, compared to just 7 per cent of Anglo parents and 11 per cent of Pasfika. This is quite a dramatic contrast, though it should be noted that, as we'll discuss in later chapters, principals and teachers (particularly those from Group 1 schools), believed the number of Chinese students attending coaching to be significantly higher. This might have been the case, but there were some issues around disclosure with some parents feeling uncomfortable acknowledging attendance given there was criticism of such activities from within some schools. But it does soften the perception that *all* Chinese students and *no-one else* attend colleges. Mak and Mak (2002) point out that they attract students from a variety of backgrounds and for various reasons – remedial assistance, test preparation and selective school entrance. It should also be pointed out that tuition might include attendance at a formal institution such as a coaching college, or it may be one-on-one help from someone at home. We should also note that the Pasifika figure seems high, but this may be because this figure might include attendance at homework centres that had been set up by schools and community organizations. Yet while Chinese background parents are more likely to use colleges as a resource for increasing educational advantages for their children, they did not hold a monopoly.

In summary, the survey revealed significant differences between the three groups. Responses from parents indicated that Chinese students not only spent more time completing homework than their Anglo and Pasifika peers but they were more likely to complete it in their bedroom or a study, working independently but generally supervised by parents. In addition, the Chinese students were given more additional work by their parents to supplement their schoolwork and were also involved far more in extracurricular activities such as learning a musical instrument or attending coaching colleges. Chinese background parents, then, are more likely to undertake forms of what Lareau calls 'concerted cultivation', representing a greater parental investment in their children's educational careers.

Parental engagement with school

One issue that emerges in the literature on the reproduction of educational capital is the confidence with which parents approach and deal with the school (Reay, 1998) which is an especially significant issue for some groups with a LBOTE (Kalantzis et al., 1990, p. 51). The survey investigated a series of questions related to parental involvement with the school as well as attitudes towards schooling. This was undertaken to establish the level of engagement and participation occurring between the school and the parents and to ascertain the degree of accessibility and lines of communication which existed. Results reveal significant findings around issues of how and what information reaches parents and parental involvement in strategic school decisions.

One crucial point needs to be made here about length of residence in Australia for those of migrant backgrounds. Arriving from another country with a different language, a different educational system and different cultural values around education would significantly shape parents' engagement with school, especially if residence in Australia was relatively brief (Cardona et al. 2009). We don't want to discount these factors, but it is important to point out that, while a small number of parents of Chinese and Pasifika background had arrived within the previous three years, most had been in Australia for some time. The average length of time in Australia for Chinese parents was 13.6 years, while for Pasifika parents it was 11 years, suggesting that most had been in Australia long enough to become acquainted with the new system.

Of the Anglo respondents, 95 per cent indicated they attended parent/teacher interviews at their child's school compared to 84 per cent of Chinese and 79 per cent of Pasifika. The numbers of parents attending parents and citizens meetings at the school were quite similar, with 20 per cent of Anglo, 17 per cent of Chinese and 21 per cent of Pasifika parents indicating they attend such meetings. Of the Anglo parents, 71 per cent attended information sessions at the school compared to 44 per cent of Chinese, although evidence from the interviews later suggested that Chinese parents were more likely to attend school information sessions which were related to academic opportunities such as OC testing and selective high schools.

Parents were also asked questions related to their child's level of achievement and their aspirations for their child, because the investments parents have in education will be reflected in different expectations. Most parents across the three groups were happy with the level of their child's academic achievement, but this varied slightly: 60 per cent of Chinese respondents said that their child's achievement was good or very good, compared to 72 per cent of Anglo parents, and 85 per cent of Pasifika parents. This means that there was a significant tendency for Chinese parents to be less enthusiastic about their children's achievements: 36 per cent were more likely to state that the level of achievement was only satisfactory compared to 24 per cent of Anglo and 16 per cent of Pasifika parents. This may suggest a higher level of expectation among Chinese parents for their children, or even a stronger perception that the school isn't quite doing enough to teach their children. This level of expectation emerges in other ways. Significantly, of those parents who responded that they would like their child to be tested for a local OC, 56 per cent of Chinese respondents stated that they expected their children to be successful in the test, compared to just 22 per cent of Anglo respondents. Interestingly, none of the Pasifika parents expected their children to be 'unsuccessful' in the OC test, but most were either unsure or did not expect their child to be tested in the first place, which seemed to corroborate findings from the interviews. Nevertheless, the survey suggested that there was a strong connection between parental attitudes, levels and forms of involvement, and student achievement, and that this was uneven among ethnically defined groups (Cardona et al., 2009).

Concluding remarks

To some extent, the survey reflected the general emphasis in the literature on the strong correlation between parents' SES (income, educational qualifications) and their children's educational attainment. It may, for example, help explain the poor academic performance of many Pasifika children who typically have a very low SES; their educational attainment may be more directly related to SES than ethnicity, or the ways they intersect. This explanation, however, proves less convincing in relation to the Chinese students. SES may have some impact on the academic performance of Chinese students but overall it seems variable. While there are exceptions, Chinese students of both high and low-SES perform well at school with a higher percentage on average gaining university entrance than those of Anglo background (Schneider and Lee, 1990; Don et al. 1995; Abboud and Kim, 2005; Wallace, 2008). Modood (2004, p. 89), for example, writing on the performance of ethnic minorities students in the United Kingdom found that more than twice the proportion of 18–24-year-old Chinese and other Asian students enter university than do whites. Also, while he found that it was generally true that a higher proportion of these minority groups had a middle-class profile, this was not universal. There was something else going on, something that researchers seemed to have missed. On the other hand, we want to avoid the increasingly common assumption that ethnicity or 'cultural values' is the explanation for these differences.

Our survey findings confirm Dandy and Nettlebeck's (2002) view that there is a complex of factors at work in the academic achievements of Chinese background students over and above other groups, including increased study time, students' educational and occupational aspirations, parents' support for studying and their aspirations, and so on. Yet the survey is a fairly blunt instrument for interrogating such complex social phenomenon: it provides broad brushstrokes of educational experiences and processes. The findings do reveal some patterns linking ethnicity with home and school experiences; patterns which will help us make sense of later findings. Some of the data received, however, is limited because it may tell us more about the parents' ideals (and anxieties) rather than their practices. But more importantly, these aren't scientific categories which represent reality (Simon and Piché, 2012); instruments such as surveys, relying as they do on broad categories, construct a version of the world. As Law (2009) argues, we 'see' like a survey because the survey has a performative function which enacts those categories as real things. This is something we must take heed of – already in the recounting of the survey data we have begun to talk of 'Chinese', 'Pasifika' and 'Anglo' parents and students as though these are natural categories. Indeed, this data suggests a seductive 'truth' to the stereotypes that circulate, especially about Chinese students.

Having made these qualifications (to which we will return), the survey results show broad tendencies which help to set the broader picture for comprehending the complex relations between home and school, ethnicity and education. These patterns go some way towards differentiating the three groups we focus on in this study: tendencies which need to be addressed by examining the detailed interview and observational data. As Bourdieu (1996) argues, it is not enough to 'have' educational capital derived from one's social class; it is about strategic 'investments' which allow families to realize social 'profits' through that capital. His notion of cultural capital is typically used to explain why dominant groups are dominant, and why disadvantaged groups are disadvantaged: it is not so helpful, as Modood (2004) points out, in explaining why some marginalized groups do better than one would have predicted on the basis of the analysis of class and racism.

Yet the kinds of educational capital we have begun to outline here are a far cry from the forms of cultural distinction (e.g. training in drama, music and art) that Bourdieu's model prioritizes (Reay, 1998, p. 51; Lareau and Weininger, 2003). These activities *do* have a strong correlation with academic achievement (Scherger and Savage, 2010), but we think there is inadequate attention paid to those forms of activity which enable educational attainment through the direct production of embodied capacities and dispositions to learning: that is, we think it important to think about such capacities not merely as practices of distinction and reproduction, but capacities brought about by parental efforts at 'concerted cultivation' that are crucial to successful participation in the education environments of western societies. With Lareau and Weininger (2003), we argue for the need for an analysis of the micro-interactional processes whereby individuals' uses of knowledge and skills interact with institutional practices, producing particular dispositions to schooling. To Modood (2004, p. 101) such a focus on practice is 'an extremely fruitful line of enquiry' and one which has often remained underexplored. The interview and observational data will help to draw out evidence of these different dispositions and lead to a better understanding of the relationship between home and school practices and differential achievement rates.

3

Disposed to learning

An increasing body of research explores the ways that educational achievement is best understood not just as the acquisition of specific cognitive abilities and content knowledge, nor as simply determined by larger social categories, such as SES, gender and ethnicity, but that it involves an array of factors which produce in students certain kinds of attributes which predispose them towards learning in different ways. An OECD (2006) report on immigrant students, for example, argued that their engagement in school can be seen in terms of a disposition towards learning which entails motivation and aspiration, self-efficacy, an ability to function in an institution, cooperating with others and a sense of 'belonging'. An Australian study similarly identified dispositional forces and barriers to staying on at school which revolved around questions of interest, motivation, self-efficacy, attitudes to and a sense of belonging in, school (Lamb et al., 2004). Research on motivational orientation within educational psychology provides further evidence for unpacking the attributes of successful learners which predispose them to scholarly work. It emphasizes the centrality of intrinsic motivation, self-determination, experiences of competence, cognitive flexibility, achievement orientation, the capacity for self-regulation, diligence and focus, and the desire to learn for its own sake (see Boggiano and Pittman, 1992; McInerney and Van Etten, 2001), as well as more specific research on the 'disposition to critical thinking' (Urdan and Giancarlo, 2001, pp. 44–5).

While useful, much of this research is undeveloped both empirically and theoretically. Its focus tends to be at a macro level, deriving generalizations from large surveys, and it mixes cognitive, physical, institutional and social dimensions, and moves too easily between the attributes of individuals and social groups, without adequately conceptualizing the relations between them. This research often finds evidence of ethnic differences in such capacities and because they are framed as psychological attributes, it seems to confirm the view that these attributes are deep-seated cultural pathologies and therefore static entities (Bloomer and Hodkinson, 2000). Tiwari et al. (2003) argue that the differences between Hong Kong Chinese and Australian students' critical thinking dispositions could be just as easily explained in terms of institutional, educational and professional factors as well as cultural background. We can infer from this that the literature is often conceptually narrow because it treats these as psychological or cognitive attributes, measured by attitudinal surveys and questionnaires, understood through reduced categories of ethnicity. Little research grapples with such dispositions observed in context, which could help to show that these dispositions may be better understood as *dynamic* entities which link meaning, action and participation (Bloomer and Hodkinson, 2000, p. 589).

Despite the emphasis on personal attributes in the research on motivational orientation, they actually translate into particular practices, capacities and values, often highlighted in the literature on motivating students: the ability to plan and monitor work, a strong sense of control and focus, a belief in the value of learning, authoritative but not authoritarian parental support, a stable and efficient work space and routines at home. Much of this comes back to the home environment in which a child studies, and not just the school experience itself. Together they produce 'academic resilience' in the student, or the capacity to deal effectively with challenges (Martin, 2003, pp. 10–11). Yet, because this literature continues to treat these as *psychological* attributes, they don't capture the sense in which they exist as *embodied* attributes derived from sociocultural practices that are learned but not simply given, and that are linked but not reduced to ethnicity.

Importantly, because these competencies are embodied they feel natural, which may explain why they are often overlooked in educational research. Bourdieu uses the concept of the 'habitus' to describe the largely unconscious dispositions which enable humans to act in particular social fields, as 'second nature'. The habitus is 'a system of dispositions to be and to do' which doesn't just embody our past but allows us to act in the future (Bourdieu, 2000, p. 150). Bourdieu's primary interest in deploying the notion of the habitus, as we have seen in relation to cultural capital, is to explain the reproduction of class relations of power through schooling systems which legitimate and reward the habitus of the privileged and powerful. However, we think that Bourdieu's framework extends well to ethnographic observation of the importance of bodily self-control in the development of capacities for writing and sustained attention needed for higher order scholarly work.

The literature outlining, extending and critiquing Bourdieu's notion of habitus in relation to education is extensive and there is little need for us to go over that ground (Grenfell and James, 1998; Nash, 1999; Reay, 2004; Reed-Danahay, 2005). For some, habitus is understood as the embodiment of the principles of the dominant social structure, yet Bourdieu is emphatic that the habitus is also generative of social action, allowing a degree of agency to human actors through the practical mastery of the social world (Bourdieu, 1990, pp. 12, 74). Despite Bourdieu's attempt to hold this tension together, both in his own work and those who take up his framework there is a tendency to use habitus in a deterministic and static way, despite the very nature of it as an acquired set of dispositions (Noble and Watkins, 2003; Watkins, 2011b). Part of the problem is that, like cultural capital, habitus is often used to do several things: to capture both the reproduction of a cultural system and a system of class inequality, to illustrate the forms of status positioning that humans undertake in the quest for distinction, and to emphasize the bodily resources and styles human develop in particular situations. These aren't, ultimately, different things, but they are difficult to hold together in analysis. But what we want to stress here is that in foregrounding the reproductive and status dimensions of habitus, the resourceful or productive nature of those capacities is lost, and we believe this aspect of habitus is actually necessary to understand the other two dimensions.

Bourdieu (1984, pp. 12–13) himself is partly to blame for this, foregrounding the relationship between educational capital and the 'cultivated disposition' in the consumption of cultural goods, while characterizing 'cultural competence' embodied through the habitus as internalizing the cultural arbitrary, or the cultural values of the dominant class. We would argue that there are forms of cultural competence – ways of seeing, knowing and doing – that are useful and powerful for effective social participation, and not simply the cultural values of the dominant class, even if they have been appropriated by the powerful (Kalantzis et al. 1989); what Nash (2002a) refers to, in contrast to the cultural arbitrary, as the educational necessary.

Bourdieu (1996, 2000) acknowledges this in his discussion of the ways the habitus we acquire through family socialization impacts upon a child's preparedness for academic endeavour, because it entails capacities that are valued and productive in educational institutions: self-discipline, the ability to work intensively, self-confidence, independence, the inclination to contemplation and abstraction, valuing excellence, and so on, but he gestures towards these without elaboration. Yet, while educational theory has begun to address the corporeal nature of schooling particularly in relation to physical education (Evans, 2004; Wright, 2004; Hills, 2007; Burrows, 2010), or as a form of social control (O'Farrell et al., 2000; Prout, 2000) it rarely considers the body's role in academic achievement. Most educational research sees achievement in cognitive terms, reflected in test results and other tasks. This chapter, in contrast, argues that scholarly activity is dependent upon bodily control, because a certain kind of stillness affords a readiness to engage in higher order activities (Watkins and Noble, 2011a).

This chapter develops this argument by drawing on the interview and observational data to consider the different dispositions towards learning students display in the classroom. Understanding these dispositions is crucial to the analysis of the scholarly habitus, the embodied capacities for educational endeavour. Rather than locating these dispositions in the innate qualities of the learner or their cultural background, we want to see them as productive *capacities* and forms of *educational capital* that emerge from specific *practices*. To do this we need to think about actual bodies in specific classrooms, and not in terms of abstracted notions of class or ethnically inscribed habitus. This chapter begins with vignettes from classrooms focusing on students that exemplify different dispositions to learning. It doesn't attempt to explain these in terms of conventional social scientific categories of ethnicity, gender, class or family socialization; rather, it tries to develop an empirical and conceptual understanding of these attributes – and specifically forms of self-discipline and composure – as embodied capacities that enable the formation of the scholarly habitus. We link this to the educational capital of the students and their parents and the students' educational outcomes, prior to the examination of home and school practices in later chapters.

Differently capacitated bodies

As this book has already indicated, a large body of academic research and government statistics demonstrate the significant variations in educational outcomes for students from different ethnic backgrounds (Partington and McCudden, 1992; Khoo and Birrell, 2002; Jones, 2005). As revealing as this literature is, it doesn't tell us much about the *experience* of students working in classrooms and how this relates to educational performance. We want to illustrate the embodied capacities exhibited by several students in our research who exemplify the range of different dispositions to learning. We do this *not* because we start with a philosophy that 'all students are individuals' – indeed, our point is that these capacities are profoundly *social* phenomena – but because these capacities are acquired by individual bodies doing specific tasks, they are therefore best understood by examining particular students in particular situations. This is not to reject the examination of the habitus in terms of structural location, but to assert, as Lahire (2010, pp. xii–xiii) does, that the analysis of the habitus needs to work 'on the individual scale', not just as an abstraction; an approach which explores action as socially complex and refuses to reduce humans to social categories. This will help us understand how capacities, dispositions and habitus are distributed unevenly in terms of patterns of practices that mediate class and cultural background.

We will begin by considering Sonia and Sonny, students in different classes at Broughton Heights PS, which was a Group 3 school with significant representations of all three target groups and demonstrates well the variation within a school population as well as across these groups. One class was an enrichment class[1] with many high-achieving students; the other had many of the *least* able students. Sonia was in the enrichment class, which was comprised mostly of students of Chinese background, with a smaller number of Vietnamese and Indian origin, and a few of Anglo background. There was one Arabic-speaking student but significantly no Pasifika students. Sonny's class was more diverse, and had many Pasifika students, with small numbers of Chinese, Arabic-speaking and Anglo students.

Sonia was a girl of Chinese background, and her approach to work was typical of the enrichment class as a whole. On one day of observation, she and her class shuffled into their classroom and sat down at their desks with minimum fuss. Many of them, like Sonia, pulled out books and read them while waiting for the teacher to enter; if they talked, it was quietly. Whether they were seated on the floor or at their desks, they sat still: Sonia's posture, like that of most of the students, was upright, even when they were working. During the observation, Sonia was almost always work-focused, or always ready to move into work; she sat still and quietly, and got on with her work; even in moments of unstructured discussion she remained task-orientated. She seemed to have a substantial investment in her work and its conduct. Sonia, like most of the students in her class, had mastered the arts of stillness, self-control and quiet. As her teacher Heather said, she was 'very motivated', 'she is very quietly driven'.

This was seen in the way Sonia and the rest of her class undertook the Year Group's maths assessment task on fractions. While other classes treated it as an everyday lesson, in Sonia's classroom it was completed in test conditions. Although many might see this as an 'inauthentic' task, Sonia and her classmates responded enthusiastically. After the teacher explained the task and the 'test' conditions, she primed them by initiating a lively discussion of fractions; but when directed, Sonia and her classmates moved easily into 'test' mode. There was little movement or talk, unless it was a question of clarification to the teacher. Most finished and moved onto their maths workbooks. There was a lively discussion afterwards as the class went through the answers and the procedures for working out the answers. There was a clear sense of a strong investment in the process and the product: many showed annoyance when they got things wrong, and deep pleasure when they were right.

Sonia, like many in her classroom, demonstrated capacities for sustained attention, self-direction and a form of bodily control or self-discipline which underlies the other capacities. We would call this a state of composure, a readiness for work (Watkins and Noble, 2011a). The teacher didn't have to check inappropriate noise or movement often – the students had internalized these behaviours as capacities that directed their work. They even policed each other. There was occasional talk, but it was rarely loud. When required, this class was capable of sustained attention, concentration and application. This was *not*, however, a class where passivity was the rule – their stillness and quiet was appropriate for specific tasks. If the activity required it, they were more than capable of lively discussion; and some of the students didn't hesitate in challenging the teacher. Their capacity for prolonged attention and application helped produce their capacity for sustained discussion.

Sonny's class, on the other hand, bustled in, taking a while to settle. Sonny, a Tongan boy, and many other students stood around chatting, playing, shoving each other until the teacher came in and ordered them to sit and be quiet. The noise from the students never abated, even as the teacher was giving instructions, and it frequently reached high levels. Sonny typified the constant movement in the room – he, like several students, frequently visited each other; one even rolled around on the floor. Sonny struggled to stay on-task for more than a couple of minutes and had little investment in his work. He generally didn't seem to care where he was at with the activity, and waited for the teacher to push him. Sonny was a large child – the teacher commented that his physical presence in the class was a constant problem and he often unintentionally bowled other students over. The teacher struggled to manage Sonny's body – he talked frequently and loudly, he constantly leant back on his chair despite being placed in a way that pinned him against a cupboard, and at a table with Chinese students who generally followed tasks, separated from the three or four unruly students.

This constant movement used up a lot of class time and signified a high degree of off-task activity: this class was in a state of decomposure. His teacher Betty said, although she thought Sonny 'has a lot of potential', 'he tends to get off-task really quickly. He is very easily distracted'. When Sonny's classmates were directed to sit at the front, several crouched, some sat away from the area, several stood. When they were at their desks, many slouched forward or leant back; many rocked back and forth. The frequent directions of the teacher to put 'feet on floor' and 'hands on heads', to call for quiet and attention had little effect, resulting in her constantly raising her voice, but to no effect. As a result, there was unproductive movement and noise, they were rarely still, posture was poor, and many students spent large amounts of time not attending to work or the teacher. They were rarely ready for work when the teacher called them to it; they saw a change in activity as a chance for distraction, movement, chatter. Despite all the talk in this classroom, these students, and especially Sonny, were less capable of engaging in sustained classroom discussion and, despite the greater emphasis on group organization, they were less capable of working collectively.

The point of this comparison is not to make a simple contrast between one ethnic stereotype and another but to begin to think of attributes as embodied capacities which differentially dispose students to learning. The comparison of these students, and their classes, shows a very uneven distribution of particular capacities.[2] Composure, or the readiness to work, is fostered by the capacities for stillness, quiet and self-restraint which also underlay the ability to give sustained attention to classroom events and to concentrate on tasks. Composure is, of course, a recognized and necessary part of musical and sporting psychology (Gordin, 1998). It refers to the ability to coordinate one's bodily movements, particularly the staying of movement in the moment before action takes place, and to the ability to have one's mind and body in a particular state of concentration and anticipation. This has applicability to educational activity, recognized in the kinds of tactics teachers use to regain students' attention. Thus to master this embodied capacity is an important aspect of the scholarly habitus. Because we live in a moment where 'activity' is educationally valued, we may misconstrue this capacity as 'passivity'. It of course links very strongly with the anxiety demonstrated, as we saw in Chapter 1, around so-called Chinese students' passivity, but this would be a serious misrecognition of what is at stake (Watkins and Noble, 2011a).

Betty seemed to licence a high degree of movement in the class, but on the other hand she clearly wanted Sonny to adopt the conduct of his Chinese classmates. At one stage in the lesson he sat bolt upright and, pointing at each of his tablemates, yelled, 'Miss, why am I sitting with all Chinese?' Betty apparently hoped that being with the quieter Chinese students Sonny would not only be out of harm's way, he might absorb the skills of application they possessed. She seemed to hope the stillness his Chinese peers displayed would permeate his body by osmosis. Academic engagement is not, however, simply a behavioural compliance which can be 'picked up' from those around us, but entails affective and cognitive modes. Sitting with his Chinese peers may have encouraged him to be quiet, and possibly even still, but a productive stillness of the nature of Sonia's would be dependent on a different kind of pedagogical arrangement in school and at home.

Such capacities are always situated and acquired (Shilling, 2004), and we should also be careful not to make a simple assumption that stillness, quiet and obedience are good, and their opposites bad (and nor should we necessarily value uncooperative behaviour as politically 'resistant'). Apart from the fact that the enrichment class showed itself capable of noisy behaviour (as when they were completing a craft activity), the point is really about the efficacy or productivity of these embodied competencies for particular tasks, and the ability to move between these capacities when necessary.

There is another kind of stillness that we found in another school. Eric attended Chestervale PS, which was favoured by parents of Chinese background. This class was by no means as unruly as Sonny's – classroom behaviour was generally well managed by the teacher and the students were fairly adept at following tasks. Eric, of Anglo background, seemed at first glance to be a well-behaved student who did his work. Watching him for several hours, however, it became obvious that for large chunks of the classroom time he did little, but was not recognized as such. He was often distracted, but not noisily, and he didn't disrupt other students. His distractions amounted to little more than staring at the contents of the shelf next to him and fidgeting. At one point Eric spent 45 minutes adding only marginally to his writing task – a comprehension exercise. This was also run in near-test-like conditions of quiet concentration, and, apart from the minor distractions, he seemed to be following the task. But close observation indicated that he completed only one or two questions in 3/4 hour. The teacher strolled around checking students' work and giving advice or praise as needed – she managed the class quite well – but seemed not to notice when she checked Eric's work that he hadn't written much. Eric, who did have a history of occasional disruptive behaviour, was acquiring a different set of capacities – skills in getting out of work that are educationally unproductive. This is not what we have described as a state of composure. Eric's strategies mean he was able to 'float' through the class, but his failure to develop productive capacities was demonstrated in his poor reading and writing levels.

We return to this classroom in a later chapter focusing on other students, but this example highlights two important points for us. First, stillness and quiet in themselves aren't signs of educational 'productivity' – such capacities always have to be seen in context, related to specific tasks and aims. Second, we should be wary of looking to ethnicity as an explanation of the uneven distribution of capacities: Eric, as an Anglo student, isn't subject to the kind of cultural pathologies usually reserved for students of particular ethnic backgrounds.

The grounding of dispositions in bodily capacities can be illustrated by considering a student in a boys-only class at Aston PS, a composite 3/4 class with a large proportion of Pasifika (mostly Samoan) students. While Kenny, also of Anglo background, was not one of our target students, he is mentioned here given the insights his example provides of a differently capacitated body. In a session on handwriting and creative writing, it was clear that Kenny had no idea about correct grip. He simply held his pencil with a clenched fist as if he had no familiarity with writing at all. He anguished over each letter and not surprisingly was the last to finish the work on the board and then made little headway with his single letters. Though difficult, inefficient and uncomfortable, it was the style he had habituated and it seemed without active intervention there was little prospect of him changing. Like other boys in this classroom, his writing demonstrated poor letter formation and uneven directionality, and very limited (and incomplete) content. The writing that Kenny produced indicated that he had not achieved the transparency of writing technology because he had not acquired writing as an effective bodily capacity. Moreover, while Kenny was not a particularly unruly student, he exhibited little enthusiasm for work – it was more a series of mechanical tasks that he was required to do, under the gaze of the teacher. He complied, but he was not evidently self-motivated in his learning; his manner did not evince a disposition to learn.

The capacities for scholarly labour

The point of these vignettes is not to simply demonstrate different abilities, but to underline several claims. First we want to stress that what we see here are *embodied* socialized capacities, not simply personality traits or psychological attributes deriving from a cultural pathology. Second, we want to stress the productivity of certain embodied competencies for particular tasks that we want to mark as scholarly labour. Third, we want to suggest that these capacities produce a broader orientation to schoolwork that we are framing as a disposition to learn. Fourth, this disposition to learn and its attendant capacities constitute the scholarly habitus.

Teachers, we found, readily drew on a range of psychologically derived categories to explain the differences in performance – they talked of 'drive' and a 'will to learn', for example – often linked to ethnic background. Yet they also often emphasized how these attributes are realized in particular, embodied characteristics – concentration and attention, distraction, fiddling, noise, etc. – which were shaped by practices both at home and school. We will return to this in a following chapter, but the point here is that in their discourse they recognized the need to move beyond psychological attributes to physical capacities and sociocultural practices.

The significance of a shift away from psychological or cognitive attributes of learners towards embodied capacities demonstrated in practices is also an important methodological shift: away from quantitative (attitude surveys and questionnaires) to qualitative research methods (interview and observation). As we saw in Chapter 2, surveys can produce useful information about broad patterns, but the kinds of capacities we are talking about here are observable, not measurable. Unlike educational psychology, we don't propose to list a specific number of discrete items which can be quantified. Rather, we wish to explore analytically the nature of these capacities and their role in dispositions to learning. When we look at the attributes foregrounded in educational psychology – intrinsic motivation, self-determination, self-regulation, concentration, and so on – they only make sense when we recognize them as particular practices in particular contexts. Bourdieu's 'practice-based' theory is again helpful because it shifts the focus away from such abstracted attributes to embodied humans in specific settings. Because Bourdieu did not elaborate his insights into educational dispositions, it is important to locate them in relation to task-related bodily competencies. *Against* Bourdieu, then, the value of thinking about the capacities for stillness is that it helps remove the concept of habitus away from a generic characterization of an embodied class history to the domain-specific action of scholarly work.

Writing, listening and talking in class are all forms of labour that require bodily control as well as forms of knowledge; it is both profoundly embodied and profoundly social (Watkins and Noble, 2011b). Sonia, for example, demonstrated capacities of quiet, stillness, attention, self-direction and self-discipline which disposed her to *engaged* learning. This state of *composure* evinces not passivity but a readiness for activity. When required, she was capable of sustained attention and application. This is not to be mistaken for docility – her stillness and quiet were productive for sustained academic engagement. In contrast, Sonny and many in his class were far from being composed; they did not have sustained capacities of stillness and quiet or, more fundamentally, the capacity for self-control in an educational environment. Sonny and many in his classroom manifested different types of bodily capacities which incline many of them, like Sonny, towards *dis*engagement. Eric, as a different case yet again, displayed a degree of quiet and stillness that was unproductive, that didn't ready him for engaged activity.

This sense of bodily control also operates at basic levels of mastery as well as readiness for intellectual activity. Indeed, such low order capacities are necessary stepping stones for higher order ones. It is very difficult to develop literacy, for example, without also mastering the physical skills of writing. Such skills require a bodily stillness and a certain posture for perfecting the technical aspects of letter and word formation. Such mastery is needed for the use of the technology of writing to become 'automatic' or 'transparent': that is, the student stops thinking about forming the letter or word with the pen, and starts concentrating on the content of what they are writing. The physical nature of the labour of writing stops being a conscious task and becomes a largely unconscious capacity, a 'second nature', which then lends itself to the development of capacities in composition, contemplation, analysis and abstraction (Watkins and Noble, 2011b). Neither Eric nor Kenny had developed that kind of mastery – of the pen or of their own bodies. Eric had 'immature fine motor skills', which affected his writing, according to his teacher, Deirdre. She pointed out that 'when your writing doesn't come easy it is going to take longer', which means he 'rarely completes things'. These 'technical' dimensions often have consequences for student motivation. At the same school, Tenille described Ian – another Anglo boy with writing and behavioural issues, as 'distracted very, very easily': 'he just doesn't have the will to really learn something new . . . his attention span is so limited'.

The technical problems of grip and posture mean that some students not only don't master writing as a developed skill, but it also impacts on their acquisition of knowledge and cognitive skills because they never acquire a sense of efficacy, control over task and sense of belonging at school – many of the features identified as central to developing a disposition towards learning. The achievement of these capacities means not only that students internalize forms of action that allow educational work to proceed, but that they also find in it and its outcomes a certain kind of pleasure which forms the basis of their disposition towards this work. The pleasure Sonia and her classmates voice is not shared by Sonny or Kenny. In fact, one of Kenny's classmates, Braydon, found the postural demands of sustained academic work a source of displeasure: he didn't like school because 'you have to sit up straight . . . hurts my back'. The struggle that some students have in completing tasks demonstrates little joy in schoolwork. The composure we describe above captures the kind of readiness that links specific capacities with a disposition to learning, an ability to move into task-relevant activity quickly and which answers the requirement of sustained attention and concentration.

These bodily capacities are thus a form of embodied capital specific to 'situated action'; that is, they relate to a particular task and context where they have value and efficacy (Shilling, 2004). Also, they are productive, phenomenological capacities for doing certain things, not simply arbitrary mechanisms of social control. The competencies we've mentioned above need close, observational analysis because they are productive for larger educational skills: just as we've seen in thinking about the writing skills of Kenny and Eric. Just as the sportsperson needs to pay attention to and work upon their technique by breaking it down into constituent components before reassembling it into fluid movement (Noble and Watkins, 2003), so too we need to break down educational 'action' into its specific components, work upon them, before bringing them into a larger whole. This also means, as educational practitioners and theorists, we need to consider seriously the 'technical' dimension of capacities as well as their 'social' dimensions (the ways they reproduce relations of power); the linking of basic literacy, bodily control and higher cognitive tasks that Sonia has mastered, and the others have not.

These forms of self-control enable concerted action. Stillness and quiet exemplify a certain type of self-disciplined restraint in which physical and mental energy are focused upon a specific task, where control of motor functions is such that fluid movement is possible, disruptions are backgrounded and elemental actions are automatized. We will return to the issue of discipline in a later chapter, but suffice it to say here that this self-discipline is not one 'attribute' among several, it is the *condition of possibility* for academic practice, similar to the qualities of restraint and industry Rosenthal and Feldman (1991) and Nash (2002) show are associated with positive educational outcomes. Sonia and her classmates exhibit this control, allowing them to work independently and with self-direction. Sonny, Eric and Kenny, in different ways, needed an enormous amount of teacher intervention just to stay on-task.

This approach allows us to shift away from seeing the habitus (and forms of capital) as a mere instrument of social reproduction, based on a principle of repetition and containment, but a dynamic and generative system of dispositions which give us agency because they provide resources for engagement in our social worlds (Hillier and Rooksby, 2005). Stillness, quiet, self-control, sustained attention and concentration, and control of writing technology, all represent capacities which produce efficacy in relation to specific tasks in the classroom environment. The kinds of engagement Sonia's class exhibited in their wide-ranging discussions reflect an intellectual agency that will prepare them for educational success.

Aspirations and educational capital

If these embodied capacities represent forms of embodied capital that enable, or disable, educational participation, they have to be placed alongside other forms of educational capital. As we've pointed out, Bourdieu uses his analysis of forms of capital to explore the reproduction of inequality in education as a process of legitimizing the powerful, rather than the production of bodies with capacities. Several decades of educational research has, however, used Bourdieu to develop a more nuanced approach to understanding the relationships between family environments and children's school-related outcomes. Marjoribanks (2005), for example, develops a model that involves a more complex conceptualization of 'family background' and the associations between various forms of cultural, social and economic capital, parents' aspirations, and cultural contexts, and specific aspects of family settings. Modood (2004) makes a similar argument in analysing the success of some students from ethnic minorities. He shows that class doesn't adequately explain the phenomenon, and speculates that we need to look at the link between parents' cultural and social capitals, aspirations and the processes whereby they pass these on to their children, a point returned to in the conclusion. Dandy and Nettelbeck (2002) have made the point in a comparison of Chinese, Vietnamese and Anglo students that the educational outcomes of Asian students can't be explained by group factors per se, but require consideration of the links between the extra time and effort spent in studying by these students, parents' expectations and support, and how these relate to student motivations and aspirations: the whole 'sociocultural package'. Aspirations are, of course, complex ensembles of hopes which can be related to education, occupation, values, etc. For those of migrant background, these aspirations are also tied up with the 'migration narrative' (Coates, 2006). Educational achievement and social mobility have been suggested to be key aspirations and strong motivators for first and second generation immigrants, yet have been relatively under-researched in Australia (McInerney et al., 1998; Dandy and Nettelbeck, 2002). The point for this section is not so wide-ranging, but simply to sketch some aspects of educational capital that correlate with the embodied capacities of the students we focused upon and its patterning in terms of ethnic background.

To make this link, we asked the students we interviewed a range of questions designed to elicit a sense of their aspirations and expectations and to capture aspects of their educational capital in formation. We asked them about future occupations, knowledge of schooling, high schools, testing and so on. In the first instance this involved asking them about what jobs they would like to have when they grew up (see Table 3.1).

Chinese students in our small sample overwhelmingly nominated occupations with tertiary qualifications, such as doctor, lawyer, teacher or vet. None identified a manual or service job. The Pasifika students, on the other hand, were much more likely to nominate manual or service occupations, including building, cleaning, sport or working in fast food outlets. Three of these students said they hadn't given it any thought at all, which in itself is an indicator of aspiration. The Anglo students were roughly divided between professional and manual/service jobs. Unsurprisingly, their choice corresponded strongly with whether they lived in a high- or low-SES area, while for the Chinese there was no such pattern, much as Modood (2004) found. The occupational 'horizons' articulated here have significant consequences for educational aspirations in the form of future training. While some of the students who nominated professional occupations and had a sense of the higher education they would need to achieve it, one Anglo girl from a low-SES background said she wanted to work in McDonald's simply because she liked the food.

TABLE 3.1 Career aspirations

Students	Professional	Manual/service	Nothing
Chinese	9	0	2
Pasifika	2	6	3
Anglo	6	7	0

While these trends tell us something about the broad orientations across ethnicity and socio-economic variation, they only give us general insights into the nature of the dispositions towards learning, so it is useful to return to the students we have already discussed, as well as referring to some of the other students. Sonny wanted to play football, while Sonia aimed to be a teacher and Eric said he'd like to be a chef or a doctor, because they were 'fun'. Eric is interesting, then, in so far as there is something of a mismatch between his choice of doctor and his academic ability, as far as we can tell from Year 3 results. His rationale, and his vagueness about his preferences, might also indicate something about the educational capital he is forming. It is one thing to have 'aspirations', it is another to have the capacity to envision them realistically and to actualize them. As Lareau (1989) has argued, possession of cultural capital has to exist alongside the ability to activate and invest one's cultural resources, and to attain a 'social profit' from that investment.

Such 'investments' entail questions of desire and pleasure in education. Eric said school was just 'okay' – the best part was sport. Braydon, from Aston PS, didn't like school – he found it 'boring'. The best part, he said, was that 'you can eat and have a rest'. Sonny liked school, but because 'I get to meet new friends'. Sonia also liked school primarily because she 'had friends to play with', but this belied her stronger educational orientation: she later talked about how English was her favourite subject and how much she liked reading. Her father Sam also mentioned the social side, but added that it was also because 'she performs well in the school'.

Choice of future high school also indicated something of their aspirations and knowledge of their options. Sonia unhesitatingly nominated one of the most successful selective schools in the state. She also indicated that she looked forward to going to university. In contrast, Braydon nominated the local high school, 'because all of my friends are going there', while Sonny talked instead of returning to Tonga to work. As he admitted, 'I don't know much high schools'. Eric could name two of the three local high schools, the nearest being the local government school, the other a prestigious private school, but he didn't mention the nearby, very successful, selective high school; yet he'd only thought about them in so far as they would entail walking home on his own. Only four students indicated a preference for attending a selective school – and all were Chinese. Two of these indicated it was because that's where the 'smart' or 'clever' kids go. Two Anglo students at Chestervale PS said they wouldn't go to the local selective school. Ian explained that: 'my mum and dad don't want me to go [there] because they don't do any sport, they only learn'. Wallace said he wouldn't go there either because 'they have too many Chinese people'.

These aspirations, of course, tell us a lot about the educational capital of these students' families. Most parents didn't wish to appear as though they were pushing their child, so often said they just wanted their child to be happy. Preferred options, however, emerged through discussion, and these tended to mirror the choices of the children. Flynn's mother, from an inner-city high-SES area, didn't 'really care what he does', but 'would like him to go to university because I would really like him to have that experience'; she thought he was 'capable' of it, but worried 'whether he will have the motivation to, in academic terms'. As well as wanting him to be happy, she wanted him to be successful, to have enough money and have meaningful relationships. The way she framed this, however, indicated certain types of values and knowledge which underlay a particular cultural capital. Joan's mother, also an Anglo but from a low-SES area, similarly framed her response in terms of the child being happy, but added, 'she can be packing shelves in Woolworth's if she is happy . . . life's too short to spend years being a doctor if that's not what you want to do'. This indicated a different horizon of possibilities and options. Joan's own preference was to work with children, but in daycare rather than a childcare organization, and she wasn't aware of the extra study needed to become a childcare worker. The Pasifika mother of Darren had as her priority that he get 'a good job', not 'a dirty job, like a factory worker'. Another Pasifika parent hoped that her daughter would get a job at Centrelink because she could use a computer.

Sonia's father Sam, a computing professional, was by no means an example of the 'force-feeding' philosophy seen to be typical of the Chinese education system (Ong, 2006) – he had sent Sonia to coaching college but had withdrawn her as he felt it was 'useless' and refrained from directing her to high status occupations: 'I don't have any, you know, sort of targets for her. I always let her chose what she wants.' Yet he had high expectations. He said, 'I expect a bit more from school', if only in terms of the time spent working: 'kids could learn a bit more if they can stay in school for longer'. He thought the school was 'a bit weak' in maths, but said he wasn't focused on grades: 'achievement is good but . . . you need to teach them how to understand'. Despite his English being somewhat stilted, Sam's vocabulary gave some indication of his own educational capital. He talked about issues around Sonia's 'pronunciation', the mixture of cultures being 'a reality' in his area, the 'social system', his 'investment' in her learning the piano, and how music helps 'brain activity' by practising the 'right brain'. Further, he felt that he could do as good a job as a coaching college.

In contrast, Braydon's father Dan displayed different levels of educational capital. Dan, who worked as a TAFE teacher, hoped that his son becomes 'something to do with electrical' or a computer technician. He'd like him to go to University but didn't think it was likely. His main goal was that 'the kids do better than what I did'. Dan seemed more concerned with issues of his son's well-being than pedagogical matters: how the staff dealt with Braydon's diabetes and experiences of bullying rather than educational outcomes. He thought 'stability' was the main role of a primary school, and he didn't believe in homework; indeed, he was happier for him to 'watch wrestling on Foxtel' or kick a football around. Braydon 'sometimes read', but his choices were Dr Seuss or Rugby League Week. Dan's reflections on his own teaching also indicate his educational capital: he was more into 'practical' aspects of his trade than 'book work'.

It's difficult to say much about Sonny's family and their educational capital, apart from what Sonny himself said. An interview was scheduled with his father on three occasions, but each time he didn't appear and no reason was given nor the school contacted. This in itself may say something about the family's lack of connection to the educational system, corroborating the general picture we get from Sonny, especially with his comment that his parents hadn't talked about high school with him, preferring him to go to Tonga to work.

The educational capital of the family emerges in other ways, such as in knowledge of the schooling system, testing, and so on. Knowledge of various tests wasn't a major discriminator among the children in terms of ethnicity, but there were a few students who had a substantial understanding of them. Flynn, an Anglo student from Colinville, said he liked doing tests because, 'I am very interested to find out the results if I got it all right.' His knowledge of the Basic Skills Tests (BST), the University of NSW (UNSW) tests and the OC selection tests reflects an awareness of options fundamental to educational capital.[3] There was a stronger pattern among the parents: Chinese and high-SES Anglo parents were more likely to have knowledge about these issues than Pasifika and low-SES Anglo parents. One of the Chinese parents at the high-SES school spoke at length about the UNSW tests, the BST and the selection test for OCs. In contrast, the mother of Eric, the Anglo boy who appeared to avoid doing much work in class, only seemed to know of such things because of what the school told her: 'I got a letter, otherwise I wouldn't have known about it.' She thought that while it would be interesting to see how Eric fared in the BST, and assumed he would do poorly in terms of the school's results, she didn't think they needed to have testing at a primary school level. Another Chinese parent at Chestervale PS was also critical of the tests, but only because she felt they should have more but smaller tests. She saw this as a strong reason for sending her child to a coaching college. Similarly, while the Anglo mother of Tilly from Allerton PS didn't want her child to do the 'competitive' UNSW tests, she was happy with more testing along the lines of the BST: 'it is needed because that's where they find out if the children are learning'.

As with testing, the Chinese and high-SES Anglo parents seemed to have knowledge of and interest in looking into the diversity of local high schools, selective high schools, specialist schools and so on. Yet many parents had quite clear opinions about local schools and their reputations, even if they were resigned to having little choice about where they sent their child. Eric's mother, in contrast to her limited knowledge of testing, spoke with some deliberation about where she would send him, and listed six different schools in the area. Significantly, several of the Pasifika parents at Allerton PS indicated they'd prefer not to send their child to the local high school because 'there are too many Islander boys there, big boys'.

But having knowledge about aspects of schooling wasn't enough. The familiarity with the institutions and cultures of schooling some parents exhibited was more likely to be translated into a greater preparedness to engage with the school. While almost all the parents we interviewed said they were comfortable approaching the school about matters that concerned them, there was a sense that Anglo parents from high-SES backgrounds were most at ease, while some Chinese and Pasifika parents felt less confident about dealing with their school. The Chinese mother of Robbie explained that she didn't feel comfortable approaching the school, because 'I just don't want to complain against the teacher; the teacher will teach whatever he or she thinks is appropriate'. Lottie's Pasifika mother was disappointed to find out that her daughter's school didn't subscribe to the UNSW tests, but felt she couldn't approach the principal to lobby for their introduction. These incidents suggest that there is more likely to be a mismatch between parents' cultural capital and the school, based partly on knowledge of the schooling system, but also based on an ease in dealing with bureaucratic organizations employing professionals. They had, as Blackledge (2001) puts it, 'the wrong sort of capital': not just having poor language resources, but not knowing how to access the information they needed, not knowing how to communicate with teachers and not having the confidence to represent their child's needs or the ability to support their children's learning.

Educational outcomes

The dispositions towards learning in evidence in both the classroom observations and the interviews are often reflected in the educational outcomes of students. We drew on the BST results in these schools not as an absolute guide to students' abilities, but as an indicator of how, at this stage, orientations to education translate into very specific outcomes, especially in testing of literacy and numeracy. Of the students we interviewed, and for whom we have BST results, the results fairly clearly show better performance among Chinese background students, especially if we draw a line between the lower Bands 1–3 and Bands 4–5 (the highest) (Table 3.2).

TABLE 3.2 Students' BST results

Students	Literacy B1–3	Literacy B4–5	Numeracy B1–3	Numeracy B4–5
Chinese	1	5	1	5
Pasifika	9	1	9	1
Anglo	10	0	8	2

More broadly speaking, across the six schools we focused on, there were some obvious patterns in terms of educational outcomes. Of the Group 1 schools of high Chinese population which also tended to be of higher-SES, one had BST averages in Band 4 (literacy) and Band 5 (numeracy), while the other was similarly high. In these schools, LBOTE students did slightly or significantly better than ESB students. Of the Group 2 schools of high Pasifika population and generally lower-SES, one averaged Band 2 (literacy) and Band 1 (numeracy) while the other averaged Band 2 in both literacy and numeracy. Of the Group 3 schools with a reasonable representation of Chinese and Pasifika groups, both averaged Band 3 in both literacy and numeracy. In one school, the LBOTE students achieved slightly better results than ESB students.

Again we can draw on specific students to illustrate these connections. In line with Sonia's stronger investment in education and the kinds of capacities she demonstrates in the classroom, she is not surprisingly a high achiever. In the BST for literacy, she was in Band 5 (the top band, representing the top 14% of students), well above her school's average in Band 3 (representing the middle 31%). She was also in Band 5 for numeracy, again above her school's average in Band 3. Further to this, Sonia received a high distinction in Science and a distinction in computing, in the UNSW tests.

In contrast, Braydon and Eric (both Anglo) and Sonny (Pasifika) fared quite poorly in the BST, again reflecting the capacities shown in the classroom. Sonny, at the same school as Sonia, was in Band 2 for literacy and for numeracy (below his school's average in both areas). Braydon's results in the BST for literacy put him in Band 1 overall (the lowest band, representing the bottom 8% of students): he was in Band 1 for both language and reading, only achieving Band 2 (the next 19% of students) for writing. His school's average was consistently in Band 2. In the numeracy test, he was also in Band 1, and again below his school's average in Band 2. Eric's results were similar – he was in Band 2 for literacy (well below his school's average in Band 4), and in Band 3 for numeracy below the school average at the top of Band 5.

Focusing on a few of the students we began with – including a middle-SES girl of Chinese background, one low-SES boy of Pasifika background and another of Anglo background – is not designed to produce any generalizable findings about class or ethnicity, but to demonstrate the links we are making between the embodied capacities of these specific students, their dispositions towards learning, the educational capital held by their families, and their educational outcomes measured by the BST results. If we turn to the teacher and parent interviews we gain a slightly broader picture.

From stereotypes to practices in time and space

The findings so far indicate that there are patterns of behaviours and outcomes which suggest that the social perceptions of Chinese background learners as educationally successful and Pasifika students as unsuccessful are well-founded. Indeed, it could be argued that we are not only replicating the stereotype by constant reference to 'Chinese' and 'Pasifika' students, but we are in fact 'proving' the stereotype. However, we want to steer clear of making universalizing claims which lead to the entrenchment of 'cultural' explanations for this pattern. This is because, as we will go on to explore, it is the practices which shape these dispositions, not the collective attribution of cultural proneness. But we also want to suggest that there is a distinction between tendencies which match cultural background, and pathological arguments that lump all members of an ethnic group together. Cultural stereotypes in terms of education have a basis in truth, but they are nevertheless myths, and not very helpful in analysing complex social phenomenon nor in guiding teaching practices.

We have seen in this chapter that when we look closely at specific students we can see strong links between particular embodied capacities, dispositions to learning and the family's educational capital. These capacities aren't the discrete and measurable attributes of psychological testing, but certain types of behaviours which are observable in classrooms. We have emphasized things like stillness and quiet for their importance in allowing for sustained attention and concentration, and have stressed the broader role of forms of bodily restraint, organization and self-discipline in the acquisition of a scholarly habitus.

We want to stress here that the scholarly habitus is not, then, a category of habitus in the way that some scholars talk about a class, gender, ethnic or institutional habitus (Reay, 2004), for example, but rather a way of indicating those who have developed the capacities for sustained scholarly work. Such categorical approaches, apart from leading to an endless array of categorizations preceding habitus, miss the point that habitus entails the *mediation* of conflicting social experiences (Atkinson, 2011), and this is the ensemble of dispositions, attitudes and perceptions that intersect in the embodied capacities of the individual as a repository of diverse and contradictory experiences of socialization and as someone who can act in a range of social domains (Lahire, 2010). This is not to say that class, gender and ethnicity are irrelevant, and don't have material consequences for educational performance, but the notion of a collectively defined 'habitus' can't adequately capture the temporal and contradictory relationship between or within these categories. As Feng-Bing (2005) argues, we can't make assumptions about a 'Chinese' habitus once we compare the experiences of students coming from Hong Kong and mainland Chinese backgrounds. Similarly, we can't assume a simple class-based coherence to habitus if middle-class students exhibit contrasting embodied strategies in schools (Meo, 2011). We need a more nuanced conceptual framework and empirically grounded analysis to explore the ways these capacities are acquired and distributed over time and in particular social spaces.

Understanding these capacities is also important because it helps us unpack the cultural stereotypes around learning which frame our perceptions of particular groups. We will explore in a later chapter how teachers perceive the ethnic backgrounds of their students, and how this shapes their practices. Suffice it to say here that the stereotypical perceptions of ethnicity need to be problematized. There are two ways to challenge such cultural stereotypes: you can 'disprove' them by illustrating the counter example, or you can understand the grain of truth in the stereotype by analysing the ways they are produced. We need now, therefore, to turn to a consideration of the practices which produce students' capacities, both at home and school.

4

Home, routine and dispositions to learning

The practices that we engage in on a regular basis from our earliest years are formative in the development of dispositions or 'ways of being' that guide our everyday life. This chapter focuses on practices within the home such as routines associated with homework, participation in extracurricular activities and parents' attitudes to their child's education as a way of examining how these dispositions are acquired. As indicated, we use the term *habitus* to denote these dispositions, and *scholarly habitus*, those that are specifically related to engagement in academic endeavour. The aim of examining these practices is to identify any patterns that could shed light on the development, or not, of a scholarly habitus which is crucial for successful participation in schooling. Certain trends have already been discussed in previous chapters. The focus in this chapter is on the processes of acquisition and habituation that take place in the home and its environs.

While a vast body of educational research emphasizes the role of the home in providing young people with the resources needed to succeed at school, surprisingly little of this research actually explores *how* this resourcing is accomplished. Indeed, as we have suggested, the notions of cultural capital and habitus are often used to black box this accomplishment, to take it as a given, a process of automatic transmission. We would suggest, however, that an array of mechanisms entailing temporal and spatial dimensions enable or disable this accomplishment. Bourdieu himself rarely discusses the 'primary socialization' of the home, hence the importance of the work of Lareau and Reay in exploring the different (largely class-based) strategies in meeting this gap. It still remains, however, an under-researched area, with little longitudinal work exploring the intergenerational transfers that occur through the interactive, everyday practices in the family; what Brannen (2006) refers to as 'cultures of transmission' or Campbell and Verna (2007) characterize as 'academic home climates'.[1] Andres' (2009) statistical analysis of the cumulative transmission of dispositions over a 15-year period is a useful quantitative addition to this literature, but tells us little of the mechanisms themselves that produce the habits necessary for educational endeavour. Here, observations in some of the students' homes and the comments of students, parents, teachers and community representatives are drawn upon to provide a more comprehensive account of academic engagement and other habituated *ways of being* within the home that influence a child's performance at school. This process, we argue, entails habits that have temporal and spatial dimensions. These habits are crucial in the formation of the habitus. Bourdieu famously distinguishes mechanical habits from the generative capacity of the habitus (Bourdieu and Wacquant, 1992, p. 122), but while we might happily separate good habits and bad habits, the habitus still rests on a process of *habituation* (Noble and Watkins, 2003). As Dewey (1930) argues, habit can be a productive force that 'furnishes us with our working capacities'. It is the accumulation of habits that is constitutive of the habitus. The task for us is to see how particular habits equip some young people but not others with the capacity for scholarly labour, and to mediate the worlds of home and school.

Habits of home and homework

Once children begin school, homework becomes a recurrent aspect of school life that intervenes in the domestic sphere. Public debates around homework surface in the media on a regular basis. Typically these reports focus on its usefulness, the amounts given, parental involvement and the degree to which homework may restrict children's free time and unstructured play especially during the primary years (ACSSO, 2007; Ferrari, 2007). There seems some agreement – though by no means consensus – that it performs an important role in high school when students need to demonstrate independent learning skills (Cooper, 1989; North and Pillay, 2002). Little thought and attention, however, is given to the ways in which these skills are acquired. The discipline to learn and work independently on a task with little or no supervision is an ability acquired over time through habituation (Noble and Watkins, 2003). Students do not simply make a conscious decision on entering high school that they need to devote more time at home and school to academic pursuits. They need to have embodied the routines that allow them to do so, much in the same way as training for success occurs in other fields, such as music or sport, through practice. In a sense, the primary years of schooling serve as a period of 'academic apprenticeship' not only in the basic skills of literacy and numeracy but in the often neglected bodily skills of application to work and independence in learning. Homework has an important role to play in relation to this and the differences that emerged between the Chinese, Pasifika and Anglo students in the timing, quantity and regularity of their homework provide interesting insights into the differential dispositions discussed in earlier chapters.

Of the 35 children interviewed in the study, 11 were of Chinese background. The amount of time these students said they devoted to homework each night ranged from 15 minutes to 2 hours, but further enquiry revealed much of this work was not actually school homework. Most students had homework distributed by their teachers on a Monday and collected on a Friday but many completed this work the night it was given or devoted minimal time to its completion during the week. Many spent longer periods of time on extra work provided by their parents or the coaching colleges they attended. Alice from Colinville PS, for example, explained that she finished her school homework in 30 minutes on a Monday night. After this she spent an additional hour on Monday and throughout the remainder of the week, including Friday night and on weekends, on her 'other work' from the coaching college she attended on Saturday mornings. Sonia, from Broughton Heights PS who featured in Chapter 3, spent an hour each night on a combination of homework from school and from books supplied by her parents. Only one of the eleven Chinese students, Norman, did not complete extra homework. Instead he spent about 15 minutes each night during the school week on homework supplied by his classroom teacher. Most of the Chinese parents felt Year 3 students should be spending at least an hour each night on homework. Norman's mother, however, felt that less than 30 minutes was sufficient at his age.

Many of the teachers of students in the study reported that it was common for parents of Chinese background to ask for extra homework for their children. As Tom, a teacher from Colinville PS, pointed out, 'If I had a dollar for every time I had an interview with a parent, a Chinese parent, that they don't seem to get enough homework, I would be able to retire now because they say it all the time'. Similarly, Tenille from Chestervale PS explained, 'I am always getting asked [by Chinese parents]. I've had a few letters at the beginning with them asking for extra homework and I've had lots of the kids ask me.' Many of the Chinese students also felt that not only did they not receive enough school homework but that it wasn't very difficult. Alice, for example, preferred her coaching homework 'because that's a bit harder'. Ben from Chestervale had a similar view: 'I need to have homework that's a bit more challenging.'

The time devoted to homework by the eleven Pasifika students ranged from one to 20 minutes, though many indicated they did not do homework each night. Six of these students attended homework centres one day a week at either their school or a local community centre but work there often involved extra tuition rather than completing school homework. In comparison to the Chinese students, those of Pasifika background spent far less time on homework during the week and on a less regular basis. They also received their homework on a Monday with some finishing it that night and then maybe reading for the remainder of the week. Unlike the Chinese students, they did not have coaching or other work provided by their parents as additional homework. Many of the teachers of the Pasifika students indicated that homework was a major problem. Kate from Broughton Heights simply said, 'Well, the Islander community don't do it . . . school is for school and as soon as they walk out of that building, that's it'. Scott from Allerton PS commented, 'there are some here and there [who do it] but it's a bit erratic'. Despite these problems with its completion, seven of the eleven Pasifika students felt they should receive more homework, as did many of their parents. A number of parents commented that they would expect their children to be doing somewhere between 30–60 minutes a night but, unlike the Chinese parents, they did not provide it themselves.

The amount of time devoted to homework by the Anglo students ranged from ten to 30 minutes, though few students completed homework on a regular basis from Monday to Thursday. Generally it was undertaken two to three nights a week with sport or other extracurricular activities intervening. With others it was even less regular. Donna, Leanne's mother from Aston PS, pointed out, it was only 'every now and then' that her daughter did it. Most of the Anglo parents tended to think that a Year 3 child should be spending somewhere between 10–30 minutes a night on homework, though two parents felt it wasn't necessary at this age at all and could simply be left until high school.

Clearly, there was a significant difference in the amount of time each of these groups of students devoted to homework each week. Despite the variance in the SES of the Chinese students, taking into account their parents' occupation and level of education, there seems to be some consistency in their approach to homework. Not only did the Chinese students spend more time completing some type of academic work at home, it was undertaken on a more regular basis than both the Pasifika and Anglo students. There seemed to be an understanding among many of the Chinese parents of the important role homework played, not simply in reinforcing skills but in the need for practice and hence the formation of habits of learning. Mary, Vincent's mother from Broughton Heights, explained that 'if he got homework he can repeat something that they teach at school . . . he will remember'. Sam, Sonia's father, had a similar view, 'First of all it gives them something to do, secondly it is not easy to remember by teaching once by the teacher, they need a bit of practice.' This focus on practice is not as evident in the comments of either the Pasifika or Anglo parents, at least not in relation to academic endeavour. The Pasifika parents, who were generally from a lower SES, seemed to see any school work as belonging more to the domain of school than home. As one of the Pasifika CLOs pointed out, '9 to 3 is the teachers. The teacher is the mother and the father, the teacher is the parent, everything is the teacher. It's got nothing to do with parents'. Another Pasifika CLO added, '[Homework] is not a priority. It is important to do your homework but they won't follow through on it.' The Anglo parents from a range of SES backgrounds had varying views but there seemed little emphasis on the need to encourage habits of learning through a consistent approach to homework at this stage of schooling, particularly among those of a low SES.

The development of a scholarly habitus is very much predicated on the embodiment of particular habits which result from daily routines devoted to academic engagement. To some extent there was little variation in the after school routines of the three groups. On arriving home from school most students had a break, which varied in length, before commencing work. A smaller number started their work immediately so they could 'get it over and done with'. Some trends in after school activity, however, were apparent. Many of the Chinese students had quite established homework routines. Debbie, whose daughter attended Colinville PS, explained that when Alice came home from school, 'She always takes one hour eating, relaxing and then she spend ½ hour doing homework and then dinner time. After dinner she do 1½ hour reading, or the other work I give her and then she play 45 minutes piano and that's another day and then she do some reading in bed until sleep.' Vincent from Broughton Heights PS also had quite a structured homework and study routine which his mother Mary explained in some detail. He has, 'A break after school until ¼ past 4, then he start his homework for one hour, sometimes 45 minutes until 5 or ¼ past and then he has a shower and dinner and then he start another time at 7.30 to 8 until he finish.'

Of course not all of the Chinese students had such formal routines. Enid, Norman's mother from Chestervale PS, explained that, 'these days he is getting on the routine himself because I just say you can finish to him first, then I will play ping pong or something else with you, because I just want him to get things done . . . Yeah he will do it by himself'. Jenny, from the same school was engaged in a range of after-school activities but her mother indicated that 'normally it will be after dinner that she will start her homework'. Despite this variation, it was clear that all the Chinese students had a homework routine: that is, a block of time set aside for homework to be completed within the home, after school most days during the week.

Homework was generally undertaken on a more ad hoc basis by the Pasifika students. As already mentioned some would complete work on a Monday but at no other time during the week. This was the case with Lottie from Allerton whose mother explained, 'Some time I ask her to leave some for another night, but when she came with the homework she did all that homework in one night.' Lacking the necessary educational capital, Lottie's mother did not think to ask the teacher for extra work or to provide some herself. Instead she was reliant on the school to monitor the amount of homework her daughter received. Joe's mother remarked that homework was 'not every night, sometimes they lazy to do homework'. One of the Pasifika CLOs of Tongan background explained many parents had 'no understanding about routine and how important it is to read . . . They don't set times to do their homework'. In relation to the students she visited at home she added, 'I could probably pick a handful that actually can do their homework by themselves without being prompted and they do it at a set time.' Clearly, many of the Pasifika students had a range of other tasks they had to perform at home after school. As many of their parents were shiftworkers, *housework* rather than *homework* was given priority. One of the school deputies explained that, 'they are responsible for younger siblings, they are responsible for getting the vegetables and the tea done; they may be responsible for getting housework and jobs done because parents are working long hours'. The establishment in recent years of homework centres for Pasifika students, some of which were operating in these students' schools, indicates there was already some recognition of the problems many Pasifika students faced in completing homework. Some discussion of these initiatives is provided below. Here the focus is simply identifying patterns of practice within the home and what these might suggest about particular dispositions towards learning.

Anglo students' homework routines were different yet again. In comparison to the Pasifika students, far more completed work at home but their approach to homework was far less routinized than their peers of Chinese background. When Marcelle, whose daughter attended Colinville, was asked to describe Melissa's homework routine she declared, 'No, I can't because every day is different!' Melissa completed homework Monday to Thursday but because of differing childcare arrangements it was undertaken in various locations at different times. Many of the Anglo students, particularly those of a higher SES, completed homework in after school care or other care arrangements. The establishment of a routine was also difficult for those involved in extracurricular activities. This was the case with Callum whose mother explained, 'We have a busy schedule with soccer training at the moment so he tends to do a lot of his homework . . . on a Monday.'

While many of the Chinese students were also involved in other activities after school, time was also set aside for homework to be completed on a regular basis. A focus on regularity rather than simply 'getting it done' was evident. Regularity established an overall positive attitude towards homework and seemed to assist in developing an understanding of its role in the development of self-discipline and the establishment of work habits. With other Anglo parents who tended to be of a low SES, but not exclusively so, there was no real expectation that their children would complete homework each night. As Netta, whose daughter attended Allerton PS, pointed out, 'It is really hard because sometimes she gets it and doesn't let me know that she's got it, which is normal but I'll go through her bag . . . and I'll say you've got homework here.' Netta tended to leave the responsibility to complete homework to her child, rather than establishing a regular routine within the home.

At one level these comments may appear as little more than random snapshots of different students' homework routines, but they can be generalized to reflect different tendencies within the three groups of students to the way homework was conducted and the emphasis given to academic engagement within the home. Dispositional tendencies are dependent on regularity of practice (Noble and Watkins, 2003). Some of the Chinese students appear to demonstrate a degree of self-regulation to undertake work and a commitment to independent work for sustained periods of time within the home environment. For some Chinese students there may be a perceived overemphasis on homework, particularly in the time devoted to extra work. This is an issue discussed in more detail in Chapter 5. What is of interest here is the apparent predilection for work that many of the Chinese students displayed which could relate to the focus given to these practices around work within the home. This is not simply a function of a particular attitude to work. For these students such a commitment to academic endeavour had become an engrained bodily practice, or what Mauss (1979) describes as a 'technique of the body'; a habit of learning forged through iterative engagement in scholarly activity within the domestic sphere. These routines aren't just organized as temporal routines, however; they also have important spatial qualities, as the literature on homework attests (Hoover-Dempsey et al., 2001).

Spatiality and corporeal congruence

Conventional academic wisdom tells us that a congruence between the cultures of the home and school is crucial to the success of many students; that is, the family values and capacities endorsing scholarly endeavour match the institutional expectations of the education system (Reschly and Christenson, 2009). In some of the work of Bourdieu and those who have taken up his framework, this has amounted to a view that schools work primarily to validate and reproduce the values, tastes and knowledge of dominant groups (Bourdieu, 1984). Bourdieu is notoriously vague about what these dominant groups are: it is variously translated by others as middle class, ruling or capitalist class, or a broader sense of a dominant cultural system. Apart from the obvious problems in assuming the comparability of these things, it would be a mistake to assume there is a simple match between educational content and class cultures. It would also be a mistake to assume that all schools reproduce the same 'culture', and it would be a mistake to assume that there is a high degree of homogeneity within classes and their 'cultures'. Despite the significance of Lareau's research, it still operates with a simple opposition between middle-class and working-class culture and, despite the acknowledgements of gradations within these categories, she often groups middle and 'upper' classes together. Moreover, she assumes a relatively straightforward alignment of middle-class culture and schooling systems.

More nuanced approaches have argued that while 'middle class cultural capital' is 'in tune' with the values and practices of school, it is more the case that middle class parents equip their children with the skills to negotiate the demands of educational settings (Gillies, 2005, p. 844). This picture becomes even more complicated when we factor in issues of ethnicity and race (Bodovski, 2010). An established body of work argues that 'cultural congruence' is a significant issue in explaining the divide between ethnically dominant and subordinate students (Au and Kawakami, 1994). Yet the evidence around the educational performance of Asian students suggests this is no longer viable as a broad claim about the relation between ethnicity and education. As we keep suggesting in this book, the desire to turn to aggregated and abstract social categories to explain complex phenomenon only gets us so far. We argue here that an emphasis on the temporal and spatial dimensions of habituated practices gives us greater empirical insight into the formation of the scholarly habitus. It allows us to examine the ways in which particular dispositions are embodied that not only promote a *cultural* congruence between home and school but one that is also *corporeal*.

Consequently, the sites where students completed their homework were investigated as well as the temporal routines. Location is significant in a number of ways. The different sites, both inside and outside the home, where this activity is undertaken suggest much about how homework is conceived and its perceived value in the process of learning. In addition to this, the dynamics of place have a major impact on a child's habitus for learning; whether, for example, homework is undertaken in a solitary or communal setting, whether or not certain types of furniture are used that encourage particular postures of learning and whether or not a place evokes an ambience that is conducive to academic engagement.

Of the eleven Chinese students, six completed their homework at a desk in their bedroom. This was not only the site their parents preferred, most of these students liked working in their room because it was quiet. As Jenny commented, 'people won't annoy you'. Homework was considered a relatively solitary activity that required silence for concentration and application. Of the remaining five students, three completed their work in their lounge room, one at the kitchen table and another in a room that had been set up as a family study which this student shared with an older brother and his father. Interestingly, of the three students who completed their homework in the lounge room, two sat at desks which had been set up for this purpose. Both of these students were from low SES backgrounds and, while there were few items of furniture in the home; it was deemed important to complete homework at a desk and to mark out a place for study within the general living area of the home. The placement and use of a desk is important in that, unlike a table, which could have multiple uses, a desk generally has a specific function. While its use may vary – as was the case with Melissa discussed below – a desk typically signifies a site of scholarly labour where work is undertaken in an independent fashion.

Of the eleven Pasifika students, five also said they completed their homework in their bedrooms. Where they differ from the Chinese students, however, is in how they used this space. Rather than sitting at a desk to complete their work, four of these students indicated that they sat on their beds which suggests a completely different posture and approach to work. Sitting on a bed to write is not a position that lends itself to sustained work. Either resting a book on one's lap or lying down to write is generally untenable for prolonged periods of time. This is not to suggest that learning does not occur in such situations, it is more a matter of considering the contexts in which dispositions to learning are formed and congruence between the academic environments of home and school. Following the pragmatic tradition of John Dewey and William James, Garrison (2002, p. 2) writes that we, 'acquire our habits from our habitat especially the norms and customs of our social habitat, our community'. There is a marked difference here between the Chinese and Pasifika students' utilization of space. The habits each acquires from their respective social habitats are suggestive of a different habitus for learning.

This is further evident in how the remaining Pasifika students used the space within their homes to complete their homework. Three of the six students used the kitchen table, two worked in their lounge room and the last student wasn't really sure where he completed homework, which seems to suggest it was only ever done on an irregular basis, if at all. Five students, therefore, did use the general living area within the home for homework yet, in each case, they sat at a table with siblings and other family members. In contrast to the more solitary arrangement of the Chinese students, school work within the homes of the Pasifika students was generally a communal, indeed social, activity with older siblings, cousins, aunts, uncles and sometimes parents providing assistance. For the Pasifika students, whose families tended to be much larger than those of the Chinese, completing homework in this way was more a matter of necessity.

This contrast in the utilization of space within the homes of these two groups of students is of relevance in terms of the formation of dispositions within the habitus. Individuals tend to acquire a degree of familiarity towards a space they inhabit on a regular basis. In a sense this marks the distinction between a notion of *space* and *place*. This familiarity, or what Seamon refers to as 'at homeness' is an embodied phenomenon that can be experienced in a range of settings: home, work, school and elsewhere. Individuals become comfortable within a particular milieu and the 'positive affective relationship' that develops and encourages a certain naturalness about activities performed there (Seamon, 2002, p. 425). Such is the case with the students described here. Many of the Chinese students seem to have acquired a naturalness to their scholarly labour; sitting and working relatively independently on a task, as it is a practice performed regularly within the familiar environment of the home. In a sense, they have embodied the posture of a scholar which allows for a particular 'corporeal congruence' between home and school. The Pasifika students have experienced a very different sense of place and 'at homeness' in relation to academic endeavour which in some respects is quite dissimilar to school, particularly in the later years of primary and beyond. While in the early years of school, students tend to sit and very often work in groups, something familiar to many of the Pasifika students from their home experience, academic engagement, especially literate practice and mathematics, is essentially an individual activity and in exam situations, exclusively so.

Highlighting the differences here in terms of space, place, corporeality and habitus is not about valorizing a particular experience or denigrating another, it is about rethinking, or 'fleshing out' what is meant by home/school congruence and more appropriately preparing students for academic endeavour which involves much more than a cognitive and social preparedness for schooling. Bourdieu's notion of cultural capital in its application to education is generally understood as a bank of knowledge and linguistic resources that typically middle class students possess and utilize to their advantage within the different contexts of schooling. Bourdieu (1986), however, also viewed cultural capital as an embodied phenomenon which is not only comprised of knowledge and language, but a certain corporeality, or set of bodily skills that is valued within a particular field. Here it is understood as a scholarly habitus or set of dispositions which is valued within educational fields. This value is not arbitrary as Bourdieu and Passernon (1990, p. 5) might claim. Rather, its value results from the way in which these skills increase the utility of bodies to act effectively in particular sites and in the performance of certain tasks: what we have elsewhere referred to, following Nash, as the 'educational necessary'. It is very much akin to Foucault's notion of discipline, though productive in an agentic rather than subjective sense. Many of the Pasifika students it seemed had embodied postures of learning quite different to those favoured at school with a habitus that was far from scholarly.

While some of the Pasifika students did school work at home, many attended homework centres at least once a week and it was only on these occasions that homework was completed. In these sites concentration was often given to extra tuition rather than work that their classroom teacher had provided. The three separate homework centres which were visited during the study operated with varying degrees of success. The Pasifika community members and teacher volunteers who staffed the centres indicated that, while there were regulars, the attendance of many students was somewhat erratic. So too, was the behaviour of students across the centres. At one located in a high school, students of a range of different ages sat at individual desks and there was a strong emphasis on quiet. Generally talk occurred only when the volunteer tutors were providing assistance to students. Any unruly students were ushered into another room where talk was allowed. At the other two centres located in primary schools, students sat in groups and there was a lot of chatter. In one centre which was divided into year groups for extra maths and English tuition students seemed to lack interest in their work and paid little attention. Many swung back and forth on their chairs and talked and joked with their friends and the volunteer tutors seemed unconcerned about this off-task behaviour. There seemed little opportunity for tutors to work effectively with students, encourage them to complete homework and develop appropriate study skills. One of the principals who was supportive of the centre operating in her school, but fully aware of its limitations, remarked that, 'some of the Pacific community kids who go to homework club never hand anything in [but] they love it, they are having a lovely time . . . they almost get hurt that you ask them about it. They'll say "Oh, I was there" but they don't understand that they actually have to hand something in now'.

Despite the various problems associated with the skill and expertise of staff, frequency of attendance, operating times, behaviour management and overall rationale, homework centres perform a valuable function in which many of the younger Pasifika students require an alternative location to home to complete homework as many of their parents work long hours and are not available to supervise on a regular basis. No matter how effective, homework centres are still sites quite separate from home. Habits of independent learning which may be encouraged in the classroom and elsewhere outside the home require reinforcement within the domestic sphere from a child's earliest years to attain the level of familiarity or 'at homeness' already discussed. Space and time set aside for school work within the home on a regular basis is of value not only in terms of a reinforcement of skills – some homework may not even appear to fulfil this function especially in the early years – but more so to encourage the embodiment of a discipline to learn on which academic success depends. This is especially important in the case of many Pasifika students, given there seemed a clear distinction between home and school. This division was remarked upon by one principal in relation to the Pasifika students in his school, 'Don't expect those kids to do homework because the need is at school, you do your work at school, you don't do your work at home.'

The Anglo students were different again in terms of where they completed their homework. Only three of the thirteen did their homework in their bedroom at a desk and two of these three indicated that at times they would also work in the kitchen or loungeroom. Another student, Melissa, had a desk in her room but she didn't use it. She generally completed her homework in a range of different childcare sites such as after school care, her grandparents' or friends' houses and so, as her mother explained, her desk had assumed another function, 'She has a desk in her room, but she is very untidy and messy and she plays too much, so there is never room on the desk for homework. I bought her a lovely pink IKEA desk and it is full of dolls and perfume and that sort of stuff, and jewellery, beautiful things that all look a mess'. If Melissa was to complete homework at home her mother added, '. . . it is the dining room table, or I've got like a big flat, a big low coffee table in the loungeroom. Yeah and on special occasions they (Melissa and her older brother) are allowed to watch the TV and do their homework at the same time'.

Of the other nine Anglo students, six did their homework in the kitchen, one in the loungeroom and two at after school care. On the rare occasion when these last two students completed school work at home it was at a bench in the kitchen. The majority of these students were completing their homework in the general living area of the home. Academic endeavour, therefore, was not necessarily framed as a solitary or dedicated practice. As with many of the Pasifika students, it could be argued that the habits of learning these students were acquiring within the home were reasonably congruent with the group-based learning environments of many primary classrooms. However, as has been mentioned, as students progress through school, academic work becomes a more individualized activity. On the whole, where and how students complete homework seems to receive little attention. Yet, given the differences that emerged here, these details could prove significant in relation to their impact on a child's habitus and general preparedness for the academic rigour required in the later years of school.

The parental gaze and promoting a productive stillness

While at high school there may be an expectation that students will complete their homework without parental supervision, in the primary years children generally need their parents to keep them on task. Many parents indicated that they supervised their children's homework in some way but there were differences among the three groups. Overall, the Chinese parents seemed to take a much stronger role in supervising homework. As one teacher explained, 'They know what their child has for homework' but more than that, as has already been discussed, many provided their children with additional homework which they also marked and discussed with their child. This was the case with Sonia and her parents with her father explaining that, 'We do have a bit of extra homework for her . . . so with this kind of homework I just mark for her or ask her to mark by herself and then we check what mistakes she makes and if she can't understand we explain to her, especially the strategies for the maths'. Another Chinese parent who felt her son, Gary, was a bit distracted when it came to doing homework pointed out that: 'If we sit with him it is better, if no, he do some homework and play something. The hand, one hand must do another thing, toy or something so you must sit with him because he is still young.' To this parent, focusing her son's attention on homework was important. Her supervision was not necessarily about assisting with the work itself – in fact there were a number of parents who had difficulty understanding the homework their child was given – it was more a matter of trying to instill a level of concentration, or the kind of 'productive stillness' discussed in Chapter 3. Completing homework for many of the Chinese parents, and academic engagement in general, was not simply about finishing the work, it was about acquiring a particular discipline; an engaged body and mind with the parental gaze functioning as a mechanism of constructive surveillance. This involvement is not merely a matter of surveillance per se, nor the blind enforcement of dumb routine. A synthesis of the extensive literature on the value of homework suggests that quality parental involvement contributes to student motivation and performance, to student attributes associated with achievement, and to parental knowledge of and connection to the culture of schooling (Hoover-Dempsey et al., 2001). The involvement of the Chinese parents represents a similar investment in the scholarly labour of the student.

Pasifika parents on the other hand were far less likely to supervise their children's homework. To a large extent this was related to a lack of understanding by many parents of the role of homework and its importance in the primary years, if not earlier, for engaging children in academic pursuits around literacy and numeracy within the home. As one of the Pasifika CLOs of Tongan background remarked, 'a lot of parents really don't understand because their kids need a lot of education before they start school and because they believe that they don't need to provide any of that beforehand. Yeah, they are really missing out when they come here [to school]'. For many Pasifika parents, however, it was more a matter of finding the time. As the same CLO pointed out, 'A lot work double shifts, so the mother will be off at work during the day, the dad's just come home at six in the morning, so he is snoozing while the kids are babysat by the TV. So there's not really any interaction, so you know, it is difficult.' Balancing work and home was an issue for Silei, Fred's mother from Broughton Heights PS. There were periods she explained when Fred's older sister was not home and there was no supervision at all so he simply had to do his homework on his own: 'That's the only way to do it because my husband gets home after 6 pm and I leave home when Fred gets home, so I try to do a bit of school work in the morning but he is so lazy in the morning when he gets up.' Problems with working shifts were also an issue for Ellie who felt very guilty about not giving her son Lua the support he desperately needed:

> I know I should stay here when he do his homework helping him for reading, but you know, my family, working and I came home, I am tired you know, come home and he come . . . I can't do this, I can't do this and this and this, so stress everything. So, sometimes when I finish talk to him and get angry I just sit down and think, you know, I feel cry, you know, because I feel guilty for what I do to him. He need my help but I am so tired.

Clearly there is anguish in Ellie's remark. She realized her son needed guidance but was unable to provide it. There were Pasifika parents, of course, who did check their children's homework. Serena, a community representative from Allerton PS, explained that with her children it was, 'the time for us to sit down together and you know, they can do their homework, they will ask for help, when I do reading, reading newspapers or something, I will be there with them, that is our quality time with them'. Serena, however, seemed more the exception than the rule. By and large, there was not a strong emphasis on supervision by Pasifika parents because of the pressures of work or simply a lack of educational capital; the appropriate personal and material resources to support their children.

Among the Anglo parents there was quite a deal of variation when it came to supervision of homework. Generally, there was less supervision within low-SES households. Braydon's Dad, whose son attended Aston PS said that he checked his son's homework at times but generally felt there was no real need for homework especially in the primary years. Donna, whose daughter Leanne attended the same school, had little to do with her homework. Leanne didn't like homework and Donna was 'sick of helping because I can't understand half the stuff that they're doing'. Byron's mother at Allerton PS also had trouble helping. She commented that, 'It is hard to sit down one-on-one with the kids, you know while they are doing it, but Yeah if he is stuck and asks, he will ask me or his Dad and one of us will help him and if I can't do it and his Dad can't, we say just you see the teacher.'

Some parents of higher SES, whose children attended after school care, also rarely supervised their child's homework as it was generally done at school. This bothered one parent, Harry, whose two children went to Chestervale PS: 'I've noticed they've been doing it at after school care and I'm not sure what's going on there. I think that they are doing it as a combined effort with a whole group of children because you can, you know, you can see that they are getting the same things wrong all the time . . . and I wonder if they are being led and not really doing their homework, they are just sitting there copying.' This comment raises a number of issues, not simply about appropriate supervision but about the nature and function of homework itself. Many parents and teachers seemed unaware of the importance of forging effective habits of learning in the early years and the important role homework can play in producing an academic home climate conducive to these habits. Of course self-discipline and effective study habits do not simply result from the completion of homework but *how*, *when* and *where* it is completed and the emphasis it is given in the home can contribute to the formation of these dispositions in the early years.

Cultures of learning outside school

In addition to routines around homework, the study also examined students' extracurricular activities, extending the survey data reported in Chapter 2. How each occupied themselves outside school and the particular cultures of learning within their homes seemed to have considerable influence on their performance at school. Academic climates aren't produced only in the space of the home but participate in a wider spatial network of activities with their own habit-forming potential. Not only were there differences between the extracurricular activities of the three groups of students, there were also gender differences within certain groups, in particular between the Pasifika girls and boys. Of the three groups, the Chinese students were the most active in terms of the number and variety of activities they engaged in outside school.

As discussed in Chapter 2, Chinese students were more likely to play musical instruments than either the Pasifika or Anglo students. Of the 11 Chinese students, six received piano tuition outside school and half of these also learnt one or two other instruments: Alice also played clarinet, Ben the violin and Yupeng the violin and recorder. Another three learnt an instrument as members of their school band. Only one of the Chinese students did not learn a musical instrument. In discussions with parents and Chinese community members, it was interesting the number who made links between playing piano and improved academic performance, making reference to aspects of 'brain theory' that drew on notions of left brain/right brain interaction. Sam, the father of Sonia who in Year 3 was about to undertake her Grade 5 piano exam, explained: 'I think basically music does help academic performance. It improves, you know, the sort of brain activity sort of thing because with piano you use two hands, with left-handed at least you practise right brain. So I think it is helpful at least in the future.' The rationale for learning piano, therefore, was not simply related to its aesthetic appeal. For many Chinese parents, there was a perceived connection with academic achievement.

Although students did not only participate in activities that their parents felt would assist them academically, there was a strong view that children needed to be doing something, that it was good to be busy and, despite differences in family income that might limit involvement in more costly pursuits, most of these students were very busy. Together with learning a musical instrument, there were those who attended drawing, dancing and Chinese language classes, and, despite the view of many teachers that few participated in extracurricular sporting activities, a range of sports: cricket, swimming, tennis, soccer, T-ball, karate and Australian Rules football. Life for many of these students was highly regulated with parents appearing to cultivate specific dispositions in their children that weren't just narrowly academic. Vincent's mother, Mary, from Broughton Heights was quite upfront about this explaining: 'when they are young we have to control them like a tree, a small tree. When they are bigger and grow up like a tree they understand what is right, what is wrong, what they can do, what they can't do'. Mary saw her son's early years as a formative period to focus on acquiring skills and values that would assist him and influence his behaviour in later years. In addition to their involvement in the range of activities discussed above, six of the Chinese students also attended academic coaching classes for three hours on a Saturday morning. Apart from one of the Pasifika students, who had only just commenced coaching, none of the Pasifika or Anglo students attended this form of extra tuition. Discussion of coaching is provided in Chapter 5, but it is mentioned here to not only provide more detail about the range of activities these students engaged in outside school but to further demonstrate the busy and highly structured nature of their everyday lives that contributed to the degree of self-discipline that many of these children displayed.

The Pasifika students, on the other hand, were far less likely to be involved in extracurricular activities. While most of the students showed a keen interest in sport, there were only four boys and none of the girls who participated in sports outside school, and in each case this was either rugby union or league. In discussing the Pasifika students' extracurricular pursuits, one of the CLOs remarked, 'a lot play rugby. Sports, anything to do with sport but they don't do anything else'. A similar view was expressed by a Pasifika CLO in another school, 'Some kids they go and play sport, some kids they go and do dancing and some kids don't bother, they just don't do anything'. The girls appeared to have less involvement in extracurricular sport than the boys. This was remarked upon by a number of teachers and CLOs. One explained that, 'with Finau's family, for example, without fail on a Tuesday and Thursday, they will take the whole family rugby training, won't miss any training at all because they love to go training, whereas I don't think they take Gillian, (who is a great sprinter) or any of the other girls to any extracurricular activities'. Three of the Pasifika girls indicated they attended community dancing classes connected with their local church but it seemed many spent much of their free time after school and on the weekend simply at home, visiting family or, as Lottie explained, 'hanging out with my cousins, seeing a movie or at the shops'.

A large part of many of the Pasifika students' and their parents' lives revolved around the church and church-related activities such as singing groups and various youth programmes. Despite the churches of different Christian denominations having a strong role in the Pasifika communities, some community representatives were critical of the emphasis many families placed on the church. One felt that 'they monopolise the time and resources in the community because everything revolves around the church'. Another was critical of the impact church-related activities had on children's education: 'our priorities are just wrong. It is important to do your homework but [many parents] won't follow through on it because we are to go to church'. Yet another community representative explained: 'family, church and community are of central importance' but felt 'that this may not transfer to education as strongly as we would like'. Apart from sport, church and the singing and dancing classes they offered, the Pasifika students seemed to spend little time involved in more structured extracurricular pastimes. For some families the cost of these activities may have been prohibitive but priority appeared to be given to family, community and church. The individual interests of the Pasifika students, therefore, were quite narrow in comparison to their peers of Chinese background.

In exploring cultural practices and the formation of dispositions to learning this differential involvement in extracurricular activities is significant. For most of the Chinese students there was an expectation that their time would be organized, that they would be *doing* something, *learning* something. The extracurricular activities they were involved in were not simply about fun. In learning a musical instrument, a language and to some extent a sport, students were acquiring additional skills together with the particular discipline required to master these, a discipline that seemed transferable to academic endeavour. The Pasifika students, particularly the boys who played rugby outside school, also needed a certain discipline to attend training and improve their skill level. This discipline, however, seemed more focused on sport;

a similar level of discipline was rarely given to academic pursuits. This may relate to the nature of the activity itself as the type of sport these students played was team-based as opposed to being an individual activity which was more the case with the Chinese students. Also, the physicality involved in playing a sport is quite different to that for playing a musical instrument, learning a language or how to paint. These last three, in particular, require a bodily composure and discipline generally more consistent with scholarly engagement. In addition to this, the number and regularity of extracurricular activities the Chinese students participated in far outweighed those of their Pasifika peers. With the Chinese there also seemed a stronger emphasis on mastering a skill, a process with possible implications for learning more generally. It was not only that the Pasifika students had a lot more free time than the Chinese, their extracurricular activities involved different disciplines of learning that seemed to have less transferability to the academic realm.

The Anglo students' pattern of involvement in extracurricular activities was different yet again. Overall, these students played more sport outside school than either the Chinese or Pasifika with 10 of the 13 indicating they did so. For six of these students – four boys and two girls – this involved some form of football with soccer being the most popular. Two students also attended gymnastics and tennis and another two swimming in summer with one of these students attending Tae Kwon Do as well. Attendance at extracurricular sport was mainly seasonal with only one student indicating involvement in both summer and winter sport, although more may have done so. Two of the students played an instrument as part of their school band, the trumpet and clarinet with only one learning an instrument, the viola, outside school. There were three students, two of whom were from low-SES backgrounds, who were not involved in any organized extracurricular activity. The Anglo students, therefore, seemed to have some regular involvement in extracurricular activities, particularly sport at certain times during the year. As with the Pasifika students, however, their overall commitment seemed far less than the Chinese who, even outside school, seemed immersed in a culture of learning.

Together with these more structured activities, students spent time outside school in more leisurely pursuits. Across the three groups of students there was a high level of computer game use with some differences in terms of gender and SES. By and large, with the exception of some of the low-SES Chinese and Pasifika boys, it was mainly the boys who played these games. Only one girl of Pasifika background indicated she liked computer games but these were educational PC games rather than the fantasy battle and car racing Playstation or X-box variety that the boys favoured. The remaining Pasifika girls referred to attending church, visiting family and shopping as regular pastimes. The boys also mentioned going to church, visiting or playing games with family members such as football and card games. In addition to computer games, the Chinese boys played soccer, watched TV and rode their bikes as regular pastimes. The Anglo boys engaged in similar activities. The girls of Chinese background referred to reading, ice-skating, swimming and playing badminton, while the Anglo girls mentioned netball, watching TV, skipping games and playing with their pets. These responses don't reveal much variation in pastimes between these students. The most significant difference was with those of Pasifika backgrounds, as a large number of both the boys and girls indicated a chief pastime was participating in family and church activities whereas none of the Chinese or Anglo students did so. Clearly church and family were of considerable importance to the Pasifika students.

Students and parents were also asked about reading practices: whether parents read to their child, what books children read at home and how often they read. Many parents whose children were having difficulty with reading felt they should read with them more regularly but those whose children were independent readers felt no real requirement to do so. The Chinese and high-SES Anglo students were more likely to read chapter books by this stage of schooling whereas the low-SES Anglo and Pasifika boys referred to reading picture books, comics, sport and factual books. A number of the Pasifika students also read the bible and bible stories on a regular basis at home. The most obvious difference in the students' reading practices related to how often they visited local libraries. Of the eleven Chinese students, eight indicated they did so on a regular basis with one student visiting his local library every Sunday. All of these students were able to name their local library and borrowed books on a regular basis. Only two of the Pasifika and three of the Anglo students visited local libraries. This difference in attendance suggests the Chinese families were placing a stronger emphasis on books and engagement in literate practice as a leisure activity as well as a scholarly one. They seemed to view regular borrowing from local libraries as significant in terms of improving their children's reading and cultivating an interest in books.

Concluding remarks

This examination of a range of practices within the home that produces an academically oriented climate reveals a number of key differences between the three groups of students. Overall, the Chinese students tended to spend far more time completing homework during the week than either the Pasifika or Anglo students. Much of this work, however, was not supplied by their classroom teachers but instead was additional work from either their parents or the coaching colleges that many attended. Differences in approaches to homework were far more pronounced than simply the amount students completed each week. There were also differences in routine, location and supervision. These factors could have a marked impact on a child's habitus for learning. Many of the Chinese students, who in Chapter 3 tended to exhibit a far greater degree of self-discipline and application in relation to school work than their Pasifika or Anglo peers, were engaged in certain practices within the home that could promote such dispositions. Many of these students didn't simply do more homework; it was undertaken on a more regular basis with space allocated within the home for this specific purpose, even within the homes of those of a low SES. The Chinese parents also seemed to be far more actively involved in monitoring their child's homework. For some parents this meant actual assistance with aspects of the work itself, for others it was simply sitting and ensuring their child stayed on-task. Whatever the case, homework was given priority and so a discipline to perform academically was embedded within their domestic routine. It was simply a way of being that these students had embodied which was not confined to academic pursuits. A discipline to learn was also evident in the number and variety of many of these students' extracurricular activities. There seemed a real imperative to be involved, to be busy, to be doing something.

It is important to stress again that the point here is not to reinforce a stereotype but to explore the formation of scholarly capacities which are distributed unevenly in terms of ethnicity and class. In numerous studies of the Chinese learner (Watkins et al., 1991; Salili, 1996; Wing On, 1996) this drive to perform is understood in psychological terms as if a particular cultural psychology produced a specific set of practices. It could be argued that the reverse is more the case; that the practices themselves are what produce the psychology with an individual's habitus mediating the process. Bourdieu (1999, p. 78) refers to the habitus as 'history turned into nature' and pinpoints a kind of 'genesis amnesia' that obscures the processual aspect of its formation; the ways in which the habitus is formed over time. Many of the Chinese students appear to possess a scholarly habitus given the particular practices they have been involved in from their earliest years. This is important in understanding the differential achievement rates of students from different ethnic backgrounds as the emphasis in terms of intervention can shift from a focus on ethnicity per se to cultural practices, and so, not who or what a students *is* but what they *do* and *how* and *where* they do it. This distinction is also significant in that, while there was some degree of uniformity in terms of the practices the Chinese students engaged in – as there was with both the Pasifika and Anglo students – they were not a homogenous group. There were differences given their individual life experiences and factors such as SES and gender which the ethnicization of academic performance and a focus on culture as product rather than process tends to mask. Assuming that a common ethnic identity signifies homogeneity not only inappropriately pigeonholes students but it may prove inadequate in meeting their individual learning needs. Patterns of practice were evident within each of the groups of students but so too was a degree of variation.

In comparison to many of the Chinese students, those of Pasifika background tended to not only do far less homework; they were also less likely to do it at home. A striking feature of the practices within many of the Pasifika households was the clear distinction between home and school. Parents tended to view school work as the responsibility of the teachers. The emphasis given to academic pursuits within the homes of Chinese students, such as establishing homework routines, providing a specific space for academic endeavour and encouraging reading, was not apparent in Pasifika households. If Pasifika students completed school work at home it was rarely undertaken within a space specifically set aside for this purpose. It was either completed within the general living area of the home, working communally with siblings or other family members, or in a relaxed fashion on the student's bed. As mentioned, this is not to denigrate this approach to learning but simply to highlight the differences and the ways in which these specific practices may impact on a child's overall disposition towards academic engagement. Finally, as the Anglo students varied far more in terms of SES, they seemed less cohesive as a group. While overall they appeared to do less homework than their Chinese counterparts, though more than the Pasifika students, the emphasis placed on completing homework, parental supervision and engagement in extracurricular activities tended to vary in terms of SES. The Anglo students of low SES tended to do less homework and had less involvement in activities than those of high SES. Across the three groups of students, while variation was evident, general patterns of practice emerged which suggest there are differential approaches to not only academic pursuits within the home but to a range of other activities that can affect a child's habitus.

5

Ethnicity and schemas of perception

The issue of home–school congruence discussed in Chapter 4 is further complicated when we think about how teachers see and respond to the ethnic diversity in their classrooms. Just as all schools are not instruments of the same 'culture', teachers themselves are active participants in the schooling process, and have a crucial role in the ways students' habitus are formed. The pedagogies that teachers employ and which impact upon students are informed by a range of understandings about how students learn and what constitutes the most effective means for meeting their learning needs. However, within the context of culturally diverse classrooms, these perspectives on learning are rarely ethnically neutral. Instead the process of learning is often ethnicized with many teachers drawing on schemas of perception that essentialize students' ethnicity assuming that they possess certain traits common to all those of a similar cultural background. Ethnic stereotypes in terms of education may have a basis in truth, but they are nevertheless myths and often border on forms of racism. Indeed, as Modood (2004) suggests, the performance of Asian students in the face of racism in the United Kingdom makes their achievements more remarkable and more complicated to explain. We are not suggesting that teachers are racist; rather, we emphasize again that the point is to examine the practices through which educational success or otherwise is accomplished. Teachers' perceptions of their students, especially around questions of ethnicity, mediate the alignment of school and home. Well-intentioned attempts to be culturally sensitive based on a multicultural ethos – to value cultural differences and to teach appropriately in regard to them – can also end up reproducing reductive cultural stereotypes.

Chapter 1 focused on the ways in which the media contributes to the ethnicization of educational achievement. In this chapter we examine the extent to which teachers have formulated similar views. We explore teachers' perceptions of the relation between ethnicity and student learning, the qualifications they make about this and the contradictory nature of some of these beliefs, and argue that these perceptions shape teaching practices. The chapter concludes by juxtaposing teachers' perceptions with their students' perspectives on teaching and learning.

Teacher attitudes towards ethnicity and education

Generally, many teachers had a sense that there were differences in the abilities and demeanor of students from different backgrounds, and differences in the attitudes to education among their parents. Carly, from Broughton Heights PS, saw quite stark differences in relation to attitudes to education: 'I don't think Islanders value education as much . . . I don't think Anglos do either and I think Chinese over-emphasise it.' Of particular significance for her was the fact that 'I don't think the Islanders understand the importance parents have in the attitudes in their children's schooling . . . they just send the child to school and it will be fine.' Chinese students were seen to 'have more of a sense of discipline within themselves, the parents have more control over them . . . a lot more control than Anglo parents'. In contrast, Pasifika students were seen to have 'a more laidback attitude to life'. As Kate pointed out, 'things like homework, reading at home, parents' involvement in education, even the kinds of ambitions of the students to succeed academically are just not as strong – that is just not really a priority for them'. Heather claimed, Pasifika students were simply 'not interested at all, just can't be bothered' and Betty even felt that,

> . . . they are not, by nature, they are not students. Some people are students and some people are not, and Islander kids tend not to be students. They are very relaxed in terms of things like their homework and their attitude towards school.

Carly complained that the Pasifika students lacked 'boundaries'. She recognized this as a 'raw generalization' but put it down to the fact that Pasifika parents 'have had no experience of schooling'. This pattern of comparisons was common across schools, as was the tendency to see each group in particular ways. It's important to recognize that ethnic categories were necessarily structured via relations of contrast. Betty also commented on the differences in capacities for self-organization between Pasifika and Chinese students. In relation to one Pasifika boy, she described how he 'just likes to be watching what everybody else is doing . . . he needs to go and get a pencil and then he will sit down and go "I need a ruler", you know. Whereas the Asian kids get in and they are very organised, they know where things are'.

On the whole, most teachers talked about the various capacities they identified as primarily coming from the home, but often saw this in relation to a particular ethnic community. Most teachers argued that Asian parents, for example, are much more likely to have higher expectations for their children. Carly said that even if Chinese parents don't speak English, 'they expect their children to be proficient in it and excel in it, because . . . if they do really well academically then they will have a better chance to get better jobs'. Islanders 'don't anticipate their kids will be lawyers and doctors. They are quite happy to be . . . blue collar workers'. Some teachers talked of the problems of having to address sometimes unrealistic expectations of the Chinese parents. Marsha said that they can be 'very ambitious' and 'very pushy': 'they want them to all grow up and be doctors and dentists . . . that's their whole idea of getting them coached and into selective schools'. Pasifika parents, on the other hand, don't 'strive for excellence' but are 'happy' with their lot.

This suggests that teachers, like others, operate with what we would call an ethnic or cultural imaginary, a set of views about the nature of ethnic groups in Australia, their perceived characteristics and the relations and differences between such groups (Noble, 2010). The issue here is not that these perceptions may be problematic or that they represent broader social attitudes, but that they have implications for the pedagogic practices teachers employed in their classrooms as professionals. Across the six schools, the teachers of each of the students, their principals, ESL teachers, CLOs and community members were all asked if they felt the students involved in the study responded better to particular styles of teaching. While some felt there were no observable differences, such as Melinda who commented that, 'it doesn't matter where they come from they are all taught the same' and Ray who felt that 'kids are kids and they will all benefit from the same thing', overwhelmingly, there was a view that students from particular backgrounds responded better to certain pedagogic modes. This was most marked in discussion of the Chinese and Pasifika students. Less emphasis was given to how students of Anglo background responded because their whiteness seemingly masked their own ethnicity such that they consequently functioned as a de-ethnicized, normative category against which other students were judged.

Schemas of perception and Chinese learners

Comments about the Chinese students were primarily obtained from staff in the Group 1 and 3 schools where there were higher concentrations of Chinese students. These students were most frequently perceived in terms of simple cultural frameworks. Overall most felt that the Chinese students favoured either a more teacher-directed approach or working independently. Keith, for example, remarked that 'our Chinese kids respond to you know, teacher at the front'. Jack was of a similar view: 'The Chinese community most certainly responds to the actual directed notion of teaching.' Laura agreed, 'the Asian children by and large like to be told what to do. They don't want to be given the free rein'. For Heather, the teacher of Sonia's enrichment class, Asian students generally tended to be more 'on-task, most of the time'. She recoiled from simple generalizations, but stated quite baldly that 'on the whole, the majority of Asian children are more amenable to discipline and direction'. They could be like 'stunned mullets: it is very disturbing to begin with'.

Generally, however, this perceived preference for teacher-directedness was viewed in a negative light with Betty pointing out that, 'I definitely think Asian children respond better to teacher-directed learning but I don't think that they are really taught to think' and Kate, who commented that 'it doesn't really teach the kids to learn for themselves'. Many teachers tended to distance themselves from these more didactic methodologies. Teacher-directedness was characterized as an approach that simply involved issuing instructions and handing out worksheets. The more positive features of teacher direction, such as scaffolding students' learning (Hammond, 2001) and guiding class discussion did not figure in the way they understood the term 'teacher direction'. It was a pedagogy many teachers believed that Chinese students preferred but that it was not in their best interests to use. It was not deemed 'appropriate pedagogy', a view Doherty and Singh (2005) found evident among tertiary educators of Chinese students who utilized techniques to increase the level of oral participation in their classes in line with what they felt typified more effective 'Western' conceptions of education that emphasized student-directed learning. Archer and Francis (2006) found secondary teachers in the United Kingdom voicing similar concerns about British-Chinese students claiming their lack of engagement in class discussion and tendency to work independently was evidence that they were learning 'in the wrong way' (Archer, 2008, p. 98).

Many teachers across the six schools associated teacher-directed learning with the academic coaching that a large proportion of the Chinese students attended outside school. The pedagogy practised in these institutions was viewed as rigid and formulaic, successful in teaching 'test-wiseness' but limited in its ability to extend students and promote higher order thinking. Laura claimed that the Chinese students would get the answer right, but weren't interested in 'the process of getting there'. Jack felt, 'It doesn't teach them the "whys" or "hows"; it teaches them this is the process, black and white, no thinking, no problem solving, no creativity'. These views evoke similar media representations of Chinese learners as unthinking automatons which Laura and Jack simply replicate despite the success of the Chinese students at their schools. The knowledge students acquired in this way was generally viewed as perfunctory rather than indicative of academic excellence with their success pathologized as a form of deviance from the norm. Tom, a teacher from Colinville PS, recounts a story about Yupeng, who solved a Mensa problem given to him by a teacher in three and a half minutes, compared to the best girl in another class who took over an hour. Yupeng was also able to explain to Tom how he did it, in contrast to the lack of understanding of process that Laura and Jack both claimed. Tom also recounted a lesson where he had his students work out a number pattern, which they did quite quickly. He then explained that there was another way this could be done but, because it was lunch time, he would come back to it later. Yupeng, however, came in after lunch having worked on the problem and told Tom that he had 'sat down under a tree and looked at it and thought'. But the punch line to this anecdote is that Tom was quite anxious about this until he found out that Yupeng had also played some handball: 'that's good, that's what I want to hear. So he didn't spend all lunch time trying to work it out'. For the teacher, the problem of Chinese overemphasis on work was at the cost of 'normal' childhood play, irrespective of the amazing feat Yupeng had accomplished, and the admirable application he'd shown in solving the problem.

The significance for exploring the ethnic imaginary held by teachers is that it constitutes a key element of their professional vision as teachers; that is, the way they perceive the key values of their craft and the conceptual tools through which they see their professional world (Noble and Watkins, 2013). This vision encodes issues around education and, in particular, questions of diversity, working through categories of identity which frame not just how students and their communities are seen, but also how educational and behavioural 'problems' are constructed. Bourdieu argues that schemas of perception are central to the habitus because they shape the actions of people. Such schemas are unconscious and naturalize the cultural categories of the social world, shaping pedagogic actions that reproduce these categories (Bourdieu, 1996, p. 73). Bourdieu focuses on the class bases of these schemas in institutional settings, but they also operate in *ethnicized* ways. While largely born of a well-intentioned, multicultural ethos of cultural recognition and inclusion, these schemas of perception facilitate the management of the culturally diverse school but they may do so in problematic ways.

Deirdre also expressed concern over the Chinese students' approach to work, 'a bright student is more a natural student and a lot of the Chinese students are tutored so sometimes you might perceive them as being bright but to me they are not'. This comment raises interesting questions about the nature of knowledge and the role of the teacher in a student's acquisition of skills. Deirdre seems to conceive of learning as a 'natural' process. No account is made of the practice and training required in the acquisition of particular skills, the need to automate certain forms of understanding which then enable higher order thinking. Overall, teachers tended to place little value on the academic coaching many Chinese students received and instead were concerned about the amount of time they spent attending these classes. Reminiscent of much of the critique of Amy Chua's approach to parenting, Betty felt that 'when they grow up they are going to regret the fact that they didn't have a childhood'. Jack also believed that, 'the sad part about the Chinese community is that they have a programmed life without giving the children the opportunity of growing up as rational, happy, contributing human beings. This was a view that Heather shared, 'These children don't have much of a childhood because they just work all the time'. Through the combination of a professional valuing of a particular image of childhood, and the ethnicized perception of coaching colleges, Chinese students' success becomes a problem.

There were teachers, however, who were less negative about academic coaching. Carly, from Broughton Heights, commented that,

> people say 'Oh, all these Asian kids are tutored'. I mean if they are only going one or two hours a week, I don't see the problem. People are quite happy to have their kids watch 20 hours of TV a week, yet these students are seen as criminal for going to tutoring two hours a week but 20 hours of TV is acceptable.

Academic coaching was also seen to interfere with school work. Some teachers felt students gave preference to their coaching homework over that provided by the school, yet there were never complaints about the Chinese students not completing their school homework. As indicated in Chapter 4, there were many students from across the three groups who said they did not receive *enough* homework from school and that what they were given was not particularly challenging. In a sense coaching homework, and the work parents supplied, filled this gap. There was also a view that many of the Chinese students who attended coaching were completing class work far too rapidly and developing an understanding of concepts well in advance of when they were introduced at school. Rather than admiring this accelerated progression, teachers were generally critical. Commenting on one student who had asked for additional work, Betty from Broughton Heights, said, 'She had done half of it in the textbook. I told her to stop otherwise she was not going to have anything to do in class time if she kept going.' Deirdre at Chestervale PS had similar experiences with her students:

> I've got kids that have done like a whole page in five minutes so it creates problems for us as well. I mean it is great that they are being tutored and it is great that they are up to Year 8 level, but really!

The completion of work beyond stage-determined syllabus outcomes seemed a common occurrence with maths. It was not only the level at which students were working that concerned teachers but the way in which many of the Chinese students approached their work. While classroom teachers favoured what they viewed as a pedagogically appropriate move from the concrete grasp of a mathematical concept prior to introducing its abstract formulation, many of the Chinese students had moved beyond this. In a number of classes, students displayed frustration at having to work through the more simplistic treatment of a concept using blocks or counters before attempting numerical notation. As Tenille remarked,

> I mean the Chinese kids love it but they didn't want to build them to find the answer because they could just look at it and do it and do it the quickest. I think it is because of tutoring and because they wouldn't really get hands-on things at tutoring.

Despite this, many teachers persisted in using more concrete techniques as they felt students did not really understand 'how' to arrive at the correct answer or at least felt they could not explain the process involved.

Indeed, coaching colleges and the more teacher-directed techniques they employed were viewed as discouraging oral participation and promoting a 'passive' approach to learning. As Keith pointed out, 'our [Chinese] kids are quite passive and just want to interact quietly'. This is a view Carly shared, 'I think the Asian kids are taught to be passive'. Passivity is one of a number of characteristics that is commonly felt to define the 'Chinese learner' along with a relative lack of learner autonomy, lack of critical thinking and reticence in class (Salili, 1996; Kember, 2000; Woodrow and Sham, 2001; Dooley, 2003; Grimshaw, 2007; McMahon, 2011). As Grimshaw (2007) argues, the Chinese learner is typically represented as 'a reduced Other', supposedly lacking skills of critical engagement, co-operative learning and contributing to discussion; abilities associated with the Western progressivist tradition of education. Yet there are contradictions inherent in this reductive conception of the Chinese student and teacher-directed learning; what Watkins and Biggs (2001) refer to as the Chinese Learner Paradox. Despite the perception of Chinese students as passive learners they are also considered self-disciplined and effective workers. As Heather remarked, 'I can admire the work ethic that they show and I think that's really important.' Similarly, while teacher-directed learning is often derided as a pedagogy, it can produce outstanding results, particularly it seems with Chinese students (Biggs, 1996). This suggests that the antipathy shown towards so-called passivity in learning and instructional pedagogies may be somewhat misguided.

Within current Western paradigms of learning 'passivity' and 'activity' are simply dichotomized. A passive learner is seen as one who is quiet, sits still and is seemingly not engaged whereas the active learner who engages in discussion with other students and perhaps moves around the classroom to access resource material is displaying involvement in the learning process. Clearly, however, either both or neither could be on task: activity through talk does not guarantee that a student is actively engaged, and sitting still and remaining quiet does not necessarily signal lack of engagement. A notion of 'situated action' is useful here as much depends on the nature and stage of a lesson as to which is more appropriate. More often than not, however, passivity is problematized, a view which seems to stem from the progressivist tradition that underpins Western pedagogy (Watkins, 2005b). The passivity many Chinese students are said to display may actually constitute active engagement in another form, namely quiet attention and concentration. A different case when the 'problem' of the quiet of Chinese students shaped pedagogical practice was the formation of a Mandarin community language class for Chinese background students at Chestervale PS. Despite no evidence that Chinese students were suffering academically, it was felt that these students needed to attend this class in order to develop their English language skills and enhance their participation within the mainstream. In fact, the parents of the students were extremely unhappy about this practice: they felt it was their job to teach their students the mother tongue. More importantly, there was some resentment that their children were being withdrawn from English and mathematics lessons to do this.

As Li (2004) explains, there are different kinds of silence and, rather than viewing speech and silence as opposites, it is better to see them as forming a continuum; an important point in understanding different stages of the learning process. Li also feels that criticism of Chinese students' tendency to be quiet reflects a lack of cross-cultural understanding that well-meaning teachers who encourage talk are not recognizing what different kinds of silence actually denote. Such a comment, however, seems to essentialize the quiet that many Chinese students display. While teachers in this study overwhelmingly commented upon Chinese students' propensity for quiet and reluctance to engage in class discussion, the classroom observations discussed in Chapter 6 provide considerable evidence to the contrary. Much like their Anglo and Pasifika peers, the Chinese students did not constitute a homogenous group. While there was some commonality in their dispositions to learning, these should not be considered as aspect of their ethnicity but rather a product of the practices they engaged in at home and elsewhere which contributed to these forms of behaviour. As Gutiérrez and Rogoff (2003, p. 19) explain we need 'to get beyond a widespread assumption that characteristics of cultural groups are located *within* individuals as "carriers" of culture'. Culture is neither inherited nor static but a lived and dynamic process responsive to the array of practices across the varying fields in which individuals participate.

The point here is not so much whether Chinese students are passive – some are and some aren't – it is more about identifying the practices that are conducive to academic engagement. Working quietly – often configured as passivity – is an approach to scholarly labour encouraged in the homes and the coaching colleges that many of the Chinese students attended. It is a form of embodiment that seems to foster a discipline to learn, a point to which we shall return in the next chapter (Watkins and Noble, 2011a). The importance of stillness and quiet and developing *all* students' capacity to concentrate may need to be given further consideration within contemporary Australian classrooms. Perhaps current paradigms of teaching and learning which simplistically conceive of active learning as dependent upon an active body as opposed to an active mind need to be rethought. As Pamela, a teacher from Allerton PS, pointed out 'I think you learn lots of things by being in your own silent space'. This was an approach to learning that many of the Chinese students displayed but, rather than inherent to their ethnicity, was among the repertoire of practices (Gutiérrez and Rogoff, 2003) they had embodied within the home and outside school that they then applied in class.

Silence on its own, however, is of little value. Students may need quiet and time to concentrate but they also need the requisite discipline and level of skill and understanding to apply themselves within that silent space. Heather, who taught Sonya's enrichment class, partly explained this in the following way:

> Some of the Chinese students excel because they are pushed and because they do all this tutoring, whereas it is felt that there are some children who are bright but because they are not directed like the Chinese children have been directed, it is not showing up as obviously.

On the one hand Heather is critical of the instructional pedagogy many of the Chinese students received at coaching college but on the other sees the importance of such an approach in promoting academic engagement; the discipline to engage in scholarly pursuits. While many teachers were critical of what they saw as the coaching colleges' narrow focus on practice and repetition, by engaging in such practices many of their students were quickly automating important skills and a level of self-direction that assisted them in other areas of their school work. As Pamela explained,

> for most people if you want to learn something you have to be shown it, you have to have it demonstrated to you, you have to have the opportunity to practice it by yourself, particularly for academic things. You don't practice it while you are having conversations with somebody else. If you are required to write or to think you are just thinking . . . as you know it's an internalised thing.

The value of iterative practice and developing habits of learning in the early years of school receives scant attention in Australian syllabus documents and teacher education (Watkins, 2005b). It is interesting to note that Dewey (1930, p. 105), an early advocate of progressivist education, was of the view that, 'in learning habits, it is possible to learn the habits of learning'. While teacher-directed pedagogies appear effective in promoting these skills they are seen as less successful in developing students' critical thinking and effective oral communication which likewise need to be scaffolded appropriately and practised regularly. Examples of this are evident in some of the vignettes of classroom practice discussed in Chapter 6. Tom, Yupeng's teacher at Colinville PS, was particularly effective in promoting these skills in his class which was comprised of a relatively high number of students from Chinese backgrounds.

Learning styles and Pasifika students

In contrast to their attitudes about Chinese students there was far less agreement among teachers about the pedagogic modes they felt Pasifika students may have preferred and which resulted in better learning outcomes. Yet multicultural schemas of perception still seemed to underlie their comments. There were some, such as Jack at Broughton Heights, who felt group work was the most effective: 'they respond better to more of a laid back approach with choices but no direction. They don't respond to structures. They respond better to feeling good about themselves and having a teacher that will relate to them as individuals'. Sypalo, a Pasifika CLO of Tongan background, had a similar view, 'I think our kids are working better when they are in groups . . . there is more activity than working in a whole group sort of thing or one on one.'

Other teachers and CLOs shared this view and drew on professional development material that was circulating in NSW schools at the time to inform their teaching which claimed, 'Pacific people are tactile and communal by nature and students actively engage in lessons that are rich in activity and involve group work' (Delmas, 2003, p. 12). In addition to making these claims about Pacific people's preference for group work, the document also pointed out that 'Homeland school experiences may have been predominantly teacher-centred with little hands-on or group learning' (Delmas, 2003, p. 12). This disjuncture between the assumed benefits of group-based learning for Pasifika students and a homeland tradition of more authoritative teaching receives little further discussion in the document as it seems to work against its progressivist bias that makes a simplistic connection between village communal life and a predisposition for group-based learning. Leaving the appropriateness of the pedagogy aside, more problematic is the essentializing of ethnicity that frames this document and its promotion of the idea of culturally specific learning styles; ideas which teachers drew on in formulating strategies for the Pasifika students in their classrooms. Yet, as with those of Chinese background, the Pasifika students were a diverse group. They had arrived in Australia from a range of very different Pacific nations and with very different family and educational backgrounds. Also, as Scott from Allerton PS, explained in relation to the Samoan students at his school, 'Some of them, their parents are Samoan but they were born here and brought up here, but they obviously still identify as Samoan but which category do you put them in?' Culture is a relatively fluid category. There may be some uniformity in terms of certain customs, language and so forth which is identifiable as a form of 'cultural coherence' but, as Modood outlines, this does not mean 'people of certain family, ethnic or geographical origins are always to be defined by their origins and indeed are supposed to be behaviourally determined by them' (Modood, 2007, p. 89). Many teachers, however, were of a different view as Sela, another Pasifika community representative of Tongan background, pointed out,

> I hear we have a specific learning style and that is the premise that a lot of teachers will work on. Because of the culture we come from they think that there is – that we have a different learning style like the sing and the dance – and the teacher uses that.

From here, it is a short step to forms of essentializing cultural pathology which effectively obscure our understandings of teaching and learning practices, not aid them. Sela saw such approaches as inequitable, 'a bit like tunnel vision' but, given the prevalence of more general notions of learning styles within educational discourse, their cultural specificity made commonsense to many teachers.

Rather than referring to the assumed learning styles of Pasifika students, other teachers emphasized what they felt Pasifika students with learning difficulties *needed,* singling out guidance and structure. Carly from Broughton Heights felt that the idea of giving the Pasifika students in her class with poor English language skills the freedom to choose what they wanted to learn was simply like living in 'kooky land'. While she used a range of strategies, she found that with group work many Pasifika students 'were not very communicative and happy to let other children in the group do the work for them'. Singh (2001) reports on Samoan educators in Queensland schools making similar comments about Pasifika children who had been socialized as Samoan. As they were far more used to traditional authoritative structures within the home, they found the communicative conventions of Australian schools unfamiliar and so would often withdraw into silence (Singh, 2001, p. 327).

If children lack the necessary skills to participate in group work, opting out is clearly a much easier and perhaps understandable course to take. Because of this, Carly preferred using pair work as she felt there was a much stronger imperative to communicate with only two students in a group, an approach she used with *all* students no matter what their ethnicity. Betty also felt Pasifika students benefited from a more structured working environment because 'some of them really need that to be able to get through the school day'. Taranga, a teacher of Samoan background agreed, 'they need structure and they need routine, that's what they need'. Jack, however, was of the view that Pasifika students 'won't respond to guidance or structure because there is a discipline required to move through that and many of them don't have that self-discipline'.

Lack of self-discipline is a charge commonly levelled against Pasifika students. Studies in the United States (Ofahengaue, 2009) and New Zealand (Nakhid, 2003) refer to teachers making similar claims. Yet, to Jack at Broughton Heights, discipline was not acquired from engaging in more structured approaches to learning but was rather a requirement for working in this way – seemingly putting the cart before the horse! Such a comment contrasts considerably with the connections many teachers made between the highly regulated lives of many Chinese students and the discipline they displayed towards learning. Clearly, as is evident in the previous chapter, the practices many of the Chinese students engaged in at home and outside school – routines around homework and the training associated with numerous extracurricular activities – instilled a discipline that had a marked impact on their performance at school. Most of the Pasifika students, however, lived very different lives outside school. As Kate pointed out, 'things like homework, reading at home, parents' involvement in education, even the kinds of ambitions of the students to succeed academically' are just not 'as strong': 'that is just not really a priority for them'. The practices in which the Pasifika students engaged seemed far less likely to engender the type of discipline required for academic endeavour suggesting schools needed to make up for this shortfall.

A more problematic example of the well-intentioned construction of the 'problem' of Pasifika students was seen at Broughton Heights PS, where they introduced a community language class for Pasifika students. Premised on the educationally valid claim that continuing development in the mother tongue, especially among younger students, would be beneficial to the development of their English language skills, this class seemed to be supported by parents and teachers alike. The flaw in the programme, however, is that Pasifika peoples, coming from a diverse array of nations with their own cultures, don't speak the same language. As a consequence, this class developed as a way of developing a 'cultural awareness' among students that they were different and that they constituted one cultural grouping. But perhaps the real harm lay in the fact that students were being withdrawn from mainstream classes to attend this class, thus missing ongoing work in basic skills in English and other disciplines.

Teacher perceptions and Anglo normativity

In these discussions with teachers about students' preferences for particular pedagogic modes they were far less likely to refer to those that Anglo students favoured. Being the culturally dominant group their ethnicity was less marked and so a perceived cultural cohesiveness was also less evident. As such, teachers were more likely to see Anglo students as 'individuals' rather than essentializing their ethnicity which was commonplace in relation to the Pasifika and Chinese students, and so were unlikely to see any 'problems' and abilities related to Anglo students in ethnic terms .

If any reference was made to the preferred learning style of Anglo students, it was generally that they performed much better at group work. As Tenille from Chestervale PS explained, 'I think the Anglo kids really enjoy the hands-on in group work'. Larissa, from Allerton PS felt her less able Anglo students 'still need that concrete work' which was conducted in groups. The Anglo kids, Kate argued, 'are happy to just kind of enjoy whatever there is . . . they are just . . . coasting along, they are not really that concerned about the academics of life'. Overall, however, no one approach to teaching was perceived as more successful with Anglo students with their ability level rather than their ethnicity determining the pedagogic approach they received. Any explanation about their academic performance instead made reference to their application, individual family experience, class or at times gender.

Perceptions and bodily capacities

While some of the teachers' comments about the relation between ethnicity and education were quite bald, they often qualified their statements, recognizing that the reality was far more complicated. As Betty said, there are 'exceptions to every rule'. Nevertheless, these broad claims about ethnicity were maintained. Kate, for example, said she was hesitant to make any bald claims – 'I wouldn't say there is any significant cultural difference' – but proceeded to outline broad differences in the ways these groups dealt with problems: Pasifika kids 'don't know what to do', Chinese kids will sort it out 'as a big group' and 'the Caucasians will just cry'. These claims are not necessarily invalid – indeed, they capture something of the uneven distribution of dispositions and the consequences for educational outcomes. One problem with such perceptions is that they universalize, as we can infer from the caveats. Such qualification implies that the teachers often acknowledge that ethnically based generalizations are problematic. Such generalizations and averages always conceal the degree of variation in outcomes and abilities. As Anita commented, 'a few of the Islander boys are doing a lot better than the ones that don't have other backgrounds'. Sela claimed that, 'there is a problem generally, lumping Pacific kids together . . . there are high achievers and there are low achievers, and there is in between'. Another problem is that these claims were also contradictory and mixed up. Carly talked about how some Asian students tend to be 'passive learners, they are not going to contribute'. Yet she bemoaned the fact that one of her Pasifika students 'tends to sit and want to do nothing'.

There is also an interesting paradox in these teachers' comments: they see a patterning of behaviours which relates to ethnicity and disadvantage, but they are aware that it is not consistent, or involves a range of cultural processes not reducible to simple generalizations about cultural background, even though they use them. What comes through, however, is an acknowledgment of the links between embodied capacities, dispositions to learning and educational capital. Deirdre cited the example of one student with a Chinese father and an 'Aussie' mother whose problems were not explained by ethnicity but by specific home practices: 'we are talking about nearly the end of Year 3 and he still can't sit in a seat and his writing is all over the page'. She listed several problems, like poor diet, but concluded that the main issue was that 'there is no structure in his life. There is no routine, he goes to bed late, he is tired, never made to read'. Laura, from the same school, commented on students' capacities as they develop at school – she had a keen eye for the bodily changes of learnt ability. She noted that as students are 'engaged they are a lot stiller . . . you can see when they've been told that they are good at something their posture changes . . . standing up straight'.

Jack, had a more elaborated understanding of the embodied dimensions required for schooling, particularly for students from 'disadvantaged groups' but without being based on assumptions about cultural heritage: 'I put having a full belly when you come to school and feeling good about yourself as being prerequisites for learning.' They can't be 'focused on the lesson, if they are focused on . . . some domestic things . . . they are just not prepared for the day'. Like Betty, Jack identified particular kinds of social skills as central to making the successful 'transition' to school life – 'the skills to get along' or being 'persistent', which helps them become 'resilient': 'Those sorts of skills . . . normally it starts at home, or it starts in the community.' For Jack, the issue was as much gender as culture and social disadvantage: '99.9% of the kids that come in because they've got a problem are boys. 99.9% are either Anglos, low socio-economic, Arabic youth, or Islander students'. But, he added, 'Never see any Chinese'.

These insights about the practices which produce these capacities are also seen in analysing the negative behaviours of students: Catriona complained that Lua, a Pasifika student from Briar Plains PS,

> tends to sit and want to do nothing. He just spends all his time focusing on other things. Doesn't want to get on with it, and I think it is just a learned behaviour. He has been doing it for such a long time it is difficult to for him to say, 'oh, I think I should get on with my work. I don't know why or how it has developed and where exactly, but he seems to be the only one . . . who after being explained something, I need to literally sit next to him and then he will still focus on his rubber, his pencil . . . it is bizarre.

Despite the fact that she doesn't know where it comes from, her account suggests it is as much to do with learned behaviours at school as with home-based ones. Scott complains that the Pasifika kids, 'just don't have any persistence': 'it is a practised quality, you can't just say here is a lesson on persistence . . . it is something that . . . has to be practised and practised and practised'.

Student attitudes to teaching and learning

Together with teachers commenting on a range of issues related to ethnicity and education, the students offered their own opinions on aspects of teaching and learning focusing primarily on the teaching styles they preferred and which they felt were the most effective. They make interesting points of comparison with the teachers' views of the students. When asked if they preferred working as a whole class, in groups or on their own, 17 of the 35 students we interviewed indicated a preference for group work. Of the 17, eight students were of Chinese background, six of Anglo background and only three were of Pasifika background. These results contrast markedly with teachers' perceptions of the preferred learning styles of each group. While the teachers suggested that Chinese students responded better to instructional methods and seemed to prefer it, many of these students actually indicated a preference for group work with friendship and sociality being the main reasons for this choice. Alice said, 'I have fun in a group because I can chat with my friends.' Gary echoed this view, 'I like a group of friends because we get to talk together a little bit.' Yupeng had a similar opinion, 'I love groups because there are friends and I would always go in a group with my friends.' Norman also preferred group work 'because if I don't know something then they will help me'. Sonya expressed a similar preference for group work for this reason.

The responses of the Pasifika students were not so much at variance with what their teachers had indicated, as there was no clear pedagogic mode they considered the most successful or that they felt the students preferred. Rather, there was a mismatch between the learning styles literature that indicated Pasifika students are 'naturally' predisposed to work in groups and the views of the students themselves. Only three of the 11 Pasifika students nominated group work as a preferred learning style. In two cases this was because other students in a group could help them with their work and with the third it was because they could assist other group members. Of the 13 Anglo students, six indicated they preferred group work offering various reasons for their opinion. As with many of the Chinese students they liked working in groups because it allowed them to work and talk with their friends. Some, such as Callum, thought it was easier to get help working this way and for Tilly it was because she could 'copy off people'.

Of the remaining 18 students who did not nominate group work, there were nine who preferred whole class instruction and seven who favoured working independently. Two students were unsure what they preferred. Of the nine who opted for whole class instruction there were three students from each of the target groups. Joan, for example, of Anglo background, said she preferred this way of working because 'you get the information better'. She didn't like group work because 'some people might not know the information and then you have to help too much'. Of those students who preferred independent study, there were four Pasifika students, two Anglo students and one Chinese student. Darren of Pasifika background liked working independently 'because it is like quiet and I can concentrate on my work'. Sonny, another Pasifika student, said he liked working 'on my own because [otherwise] everybody bothers me when I work'. Flynn, a student of Anglo background, preferred working on his own rather than in groups because 'I want to make my own decisions. When I am working in a group all the other people in my group make other decisions.'

While these responses provide some insight into the students' learning within a classroom context, what proved more interesting was their opinions about how they felt they learnt best. Only two students who had nominated whole-class instruction or working independently for the previous question changed their response. Both of these students had nominated whole class instruction as their preferred learning style but felt that they learned better when working independently. One of these students was of Anglo background and the other, Lottie, was a Pasifika student who said, 'Well, it is just that I like to think to myself!' Of the 17 students who had opted for group work, only one, Ben, a Chinese student, had indicated this was the way he felt he learnt best. He explained that, 'If you do it by yourself you just get bored and when you get bored you lose more concentration.' Interestingly, working with others was the way Ben felt he kept on-task. For the remaining 16 students who had indicated a preference for group work, this was not the case. While group work allowed them to talk to their friends and receive help, they felt they learnt much better either working independently or with the whole class. Alice of Chinese background, thought she learnt better, 'when we sit on the floor and listen to the teacher'. Vincent, also of Chinese background, liked whole class instruction because 'It's faster and we don't waste time.'

Woodrow and Sham's survey of 150 British-Chinese students and 200 British-European students (aged 11–16) yielded some similar but also contrasting results. Rather than making a distinction between how students preferred to work and how best they felt they learned, Woodrow and Sham (2001) focused on the former and found 84 per cent of the British-Chinese students preferred to work on their own whereas 77 per cent of the British-European preferred group work. Though a much smaller and younger sample and using interviews rather than a survey, the differences between the Chinese, Pasifika and Anglo students in our study in terms of a preferred pedagogic mode was far less obvious. If anything there was a greater tendency for the Chinese students to prefer working in groups. What was significant was how most of these students changed their response when they were asked about how they best learned. Most opted for working independently but so too did most of the Pasifika and Anglo students.

Woodrow and Sham's study seems to confirm the stereotype of the uncommunicative and passive Chinese learner. Despite surveying British-Chinese students who were either born in the United Kingdom or second- and third-generation immigrants, they concluded that these students appeared 'to live in a cocoon within British society'. Francis and Archer (2005), however, critique these findings and suggest that the British-Chinese students may have even constructed themselves in this way in survey responses and felt detailed classroom observation would yield more nuanced results that challenge this stereotype. Woodrow and Sham indicate that they also undertook classroom observation which supports these findings but no ethnographic description is provided. Either way, the Chinese background students in our study who were either first or second generation immigrants, with some also being relatively recent arrivals, seemed happy to both participate in class discussion and work quietly. Much depended on the nature and stage of a lesson and the degree to which their teachers promoted and scaffolded this aspect of their learning. Most indicated they enjoyed the sociality of group work but, with the exception of Ben, felt it hindered their ability to concentrate. When they had to complete a task they felt it was best done independently. Thea, one of the teachers at Chestervale PS, remarked upon this with her class of predominantly Chinese students:

The classroom is buzzing and there is talk and there is you know all these things going on and then all of a sudden you hand them the sheet, they go to their seats and there is dead quiet. I could leave them with three sheets of work and they would plough through them and there wouldn't be a sound and they would keep going. It is almost like you switch on a button. They regard that as real work . . . So they have this concept of what work is.

Unlike the stereotype of the passive Chinese learner, Thea's students participated well in class and group discussion but when they were required to complete a task individually they had sufficient self-discipline to switch modes easily, self-regulating their behaviour to match the required approach to learning.

As a group the Pasifika students were also more likely to indicate that they learnt best by working independently. There were few accounts from teachers, however, that mentioned this ability. This may suggest that while many of these students felt they worked better this way they actually had difficulty doing so. As with many of the lower SES Anglo students, they lacked the necessary discipline that so many of the Chinese students had embodied as a function of the patterns of practices which they had engaged in outside school. This was not only the additional academic coaching, as not all the Chinese students attended these classes, but most were completing additional homework or had routines that involved regular practice that prepared them for working independently at school.

Overall, many students indicated there was far too much emphasis on group work in class. It may be a useful pedagogic approach for encouraging discussion and co-operation, but it seemed that insufficient time was devoted to either whole-class instruction or the quiet, time and space for students to work independently. The latter does not simply involve leaving students to work on their own but for teachers to scaffold the required independent learning skills to enable them to do so. While this was not an issue for many of the Chinese students, it seemed of particular importance for many of the Pasifika students and those of a low-SES Anglo background. The practices within their domestic environments were far less likely to instil these dispositions which were so necessary for the successful completion of the work they undertook in class.

Concluding remarks

We have shown that while some teachers are careful of over-generalization, and display interesting insights into the complexities of the links between ethnicity and educational experience, behaviour and performance, they still tend to perceive these links in fairly reductive ways which are often at odds with the views of their students. The teachers articulate a professional vision premised on a multicultural schema of perceptions. As a result, they make broad and often contradictory generalizations on the basis of cultural pathology, even if they acknowledge their problematic nature. More importantly, there is also acknowledgment that, despite often resting on assumptions about the biological or cultural inevitability of these capacities, they are in fact reproduced through specific practices at home and school. As we've suggested, even well-intentioned attempts to be culturally sensitive can end up reproducing constrictive stereotypes and questionable educational programmes designed to address perceived needs. As a consequence, they need to be problematized. In Chapter 4 we explored how practices in the home contribute to students' dispositions to learn. We now turn to the school to examine the ways in which whole school and classroom practices are similarly formative in the dispositions to learning that these students display.

6

Schools, pedagogy and discipline

It is, of course, a truism to state that practises within the school are formative in the development of dispositions to learning among students. Yet despite decades of research in schools, *how* this is achieved often remains a source of debate. Central to this is the question of discipline. Throughout this book we have pointed to the importance of self-discipline in the formation of capacities for scholarly endeavour. Between an academic emphasis on discipline as a mode of subjection and the pragmatic focus on discipline as a technique of classroom management, we wish to assert the need to think differently, and more complexly, about the form and function of discipline. Following the previous chapter's focus on teachers' perceptions of difference, this chapter considers the ways in which individual school cultures and classroom practices engender forms of embodiment that contribute to the different dispositions to learning of the students from Chinese, Pasifika and Anglo backgrounds discussed in this book. This is undertaken through an examination of the classroom experiences of a selection of these students from the six schools focusing on an analysis of the organization and regimen of their schools and classrooms and the techniques their teachers employ in managing the culture of the school and implementing the curriculum. It becomes clear that these constitute different disciplinary modes working upon different axes of engagement and control. These diverse modes have varying effects that either augment dispositions to learning acquired within the home or simply reinforce students' existing habitus which may or may not dispose them to learn.

Assembled bodies and spatial disciplining

Spaces always exude a certain ambience and schools are no different. As institutional settings they will often actively cultivate a particular ethos by promoting certain practices related to organization, discipline, academic programmes, extracurricular activities, uniform and the school environment (Atkinson, 2011, p. 342). Of course SES and other factors such as a school's geographical location, architectural layout, resources, private/public status and the sociocultural make-up of its student population impact upon these. It is not the intent here to profile each school but rather to highlight one aspect of school culture that provides some insight into student conduct and academic engagement, each of which is central to the formation of a scholarly habitus. As examples of the collective make-up of a school, assemblies prove especially useful in this regard. They differ in terms of when and where they are held and their overall purpose and content. Here we examine two quite different assemblies their content, organization, expectations of students' conduct and how the combination of these produced a particular ambience indicative it seemed of each school's culture.

The first assembly was quite a formal affair conducted on a Friday morning at Colinville PS immediately after roll call. This was a regular weekly assembly for Years 3–6 students and this particular day was very cold and wet. Despite this, students followed an orderly routine of forwarding into the school hall accompanied by their class teacher. Each class sat on the wooden floor in their predetermined position waiting for the assembly to commence. Although there was little noise and restlessness one executive staff member indicated to students that quiet was required by clapping his hands a number of times. Following this, there was absolute quiet and he introduced the Year 5 class that was hosting the assembly. A class representative opened proceedings with an Acknowledgement of Country – a practice recognizing the original Aboriginal owners of the land – and then introduced the Principal for his address to the school. The Principal commenced by referring to a range of school achievements including a performance at the Sydney Opera House the previous night. This was followed by a series of class awards for effort and academic achievement and then some impressive presentations by the host class on group assignments they had recently completed including a powerpoint presentation projected on a large screen involving music and animation. The staff member overseeing the assembly also announced the names of students who had been collecting money for charity, and ribbons were distributed by House Captains to students who had excelled in sport. All these students were greeted with applause from the audience. There were a number of other announcements and the assembly finally concluded with a performance by the choir, the national anthem and an award for the class of the week.

In all, approximately 450 students managed to sit quietly and listen to the proceedings for a period of 1¼ hours. Generally these assemblies were a little shorter but there was much to acknowledge on this occasion. During this time, with students seated cross-legged on the wooden floor, there was very little noise or restlessness. There had been no need after the initial call for quiet to regain students' attention and correct behaviour. There simply seemed an expectation that students would behave and they did. They seemed to have embodied the necessary discipline to control their bodies and conduct themselves appropriately with staff standing or sitting on chairs throughout the hall to ensure this order was maintained. Their presence did not suggest an overt surveillance; rather, there was a collective expectation of order and this appeared to be all that was required to sustain the appropriate conduct of the assembled student body. Of interest here is not just the organization and student behaviour but the assembly's overall purpose. There was a definite focus on achievement at various levels: school, class and individual and in a range of fields such as academic, sport, performing arts and extracurricular activities. It wasn't simply a matter of singling out individual students' achievement but of creating a sense of inclusion and whole school involvement that translated into what appeared to be a genuine interest in proceedings with the mass of students sharing this sense of success. The assembly was suggestive of a vibrant and dynamic school culture that seemed to engender a discipline of engagement among students, regulating their behaviour and performance at school.

This was in stark contrast to another assembly held at Aston PS which was a regular daily event occurring immediately after the morning bell and prior to students forwarding to class. Given the regularity of the assembly one would assume set routines about conduct and organization were in place. To some extent this was the case. Students stood in class groups in the main quadrangle, some accompanied by teachers. There were also many parents and students' younger siblings milling around. An executive staff member held a portable loud speaker on a raised platform and called for quiet. This, however, was never achieved. Throughout the ten-minute assembly there was constant noise and chatter. Despite the teacher in charge and others issuing numerous reprimands that resulted in moments of reduced noise, the chatter and restless behaviour soon returned and the staff member in charge simply continued addressing the assembly relaying notices and calling for others to do so. Messages included reminders about school events, calls for involvement in particular activities and a notice drawing students' attention to the daily detention list that would be distributed via the school intercom system later in the morning. Following this, students forwarded to class in a rowdy fashion never really checking their behaviour despite the presence of their teachers, other staff and also many parents. This was the way students started their school day assuming a form of comportment that exhibited indifference or at least a lack of the control required for meaningful engagement in learning. Students seemed to have embodied a discipline of disengagement. There appeared to be no real expectation of quiet and orderly conduct and so none was given. This assembly of course had a very different function to that described at Colinville PS. It was about communicating information but its success in doing so, given the inattention of the students, seemed negligible. Aston PS also held assemblies where the focus was recognition of achievement but on a less regular basis. As a similar approach to the daily assembly was evident each time it was observed, conduct on more formal occasions may not have been much different.

The daily assemblies at Aston PS seemed to evoke a culture of indifference to the extent that even reminders about detention had little effect. The disciplinary apparatus at the school simply reinforced the culture of disengagement and attempts at control were generally ineffectual. One new staff member referred to the school as having a culture that was 'punitive' and that some staff felt that 'if we are not punitive then we are not doing our job'. This approach was amplified by the daily intercom announcements of recess and lunchtime detentions that listed approximately 10–15 students who were required to attend. Another new member of staff commented that, 'I think the teachers' point of view is it is good because it is sort of shaming them but I think maybe from the kids' point of view it is a prestige thing.' These techniques, therefore, were proving counterproductive, encouraging a habitus of resistance rather than engagement in learning. The reason for comparing these two school assemblies, however, is not to simply characterize one as successful and the other as experiencing problems but rather to demonstrate how different cultures of schooling have different disciplinary effects that impact on students' bodies and minds and ultimately their performance at school.

Although each school was profiled in the Introduction, given the difference between these two assemblies it is pertinent to revisit the make-up of each of these schools' student populations. Colinville PS, where the first assembly was held, has a large proportion of Chinese students. Many, but by no means all, are of a higher SES as were a considerable number of other students at the school. Aston PS was located in a low-SES area with a large number of students from Pasifika backgrounds. Experiences of school for these two groups of students were quite different, impacting markedly on their habitus for learning. The class context of each school tells us something about the situation in which these practices emerge and have effect, but not much about *how* and *to what effect* these practices shape students' performance at school and school culture. The professional literature reminds us that through the programmes they implement and the structures they put in place, it is possible for schools to not only promote a positive ethos but to improve student outcomes. Schools can act as agents of change and augment the capacities students acquire within the home. Without the appropriate intervention, however, schools only serve to reproduce a child's existing habitus which may not be conducive to academic endeavour.

Academic sociologies of schooling might damn Colinville as an instance of class-based subjection and reproduction, and perhaps valorize Aston as a form of working-class resistance, but neither caricature would do justice to the forms of social organization they represent. We suggest that these examples allow us to think much more complexly about the nature of discipline in schools. The ordered school assembly for some might reflect a harsh work ethic functional to capitalist economies and governmental control, with discipline placed in opposition to freedom, a loss of agency and something to be resisted (Preston and Symes, 1994, pp. 40–2, 135). Foucault, who included schools in his discussion of disciplinary regimes in modern institutions, had a more nuanced understanding of discipline. He insisted on the productive and enabling nature of discipline: it 'is no longer simply an art of distributing bodies . . . but of composing forces in order to obtain an efficient machine'. To Foucault (1977, p. 136), a 'docile' body is one 'that may be subjected, used, transformed and improved' but it is useful because it is *skilled*. For a body to operate as a mechanism with effective capacities, it must assume a position of docility to allow disciplinary processes to shape and skill it to perform specific tasks. This is a routinized process of surveillance and training that may appear to constitute what Foucault later reduces to a simple 'morality of obedience' (1977, pp. 164–7), but it also produces the *self-control* of physical movement and sustained attention which allows humans to actively appropriate disciplinary power for their own ends (Watkins, 2011b). This is not to ignore the role of discipline in the functioning of power nor the oppressive nature of some forms of disciplinary regimes – indeed, it is crucial that we recognize multiple forms of discipline and the diverse relations they have to reproducing or transforming the habitus of human subjects. This involves not just a more 'productive' view of discipline, but opens up a space for articulating the *pedagogical* relations of disciplinary processes, a neglected aspect of subjectivity.

School assemblies, then, provide just a brief glimpse into one aspect of the disciplinary order of school culture; practices in which students engage on a day-to-day basis in classrooms, however, have a greater impact and it is these that are examined in a series of the vignettes below. Thirty-five students in 18 classrooms across six schools were observed during the course of this study. Here we focus on six of these classrooms which exemplify the range of practice that was evident. It is not only how teachers implemented the curriculum that is considered but how they organized their classroom and the regimen they created. Each of these factors has a powerful influence on a child's habitus for learning by engendering differing degrees or modalities of discipline (Watkins, 2010). These modalities of discipline appeared to function in four distinct ways as:

- a disabling discipline of control;
- an enabling discipline of control;
- a discipline of disengagement;
- a discipline of engagement.

This analysis of classroom practice highlights the complex micropractices that are constitutive of these disciplinary modes which in turn contribute to the formation of the different dispositions to learning that the students of Chinese, Pasifika and Anglo backgrounds display. While the techniques observed during these individual lessons may not be indicative of each teacher's overall practice, they do provide the means by which practice can be analysed providing qualitative insights into the complexities of different classroom environments.

Ben, Walter and Eric – A discipline of control and unproductive quietness

3A was a class of 29 students at Chestervale PS of which 70 per cent were from a LBOTE. Twenty-five of the students were from either a Chinese or Korean background, three were of an Indian background and there was one Anglo student. Three students in the class were involved in the study: Ben and Walter of Chinese background and Eric who was the sole Anglo student in the class. Eric, who was discussed in Chapter 3, and Ben were from relatively high SES backgrounds whereas Walter's family was far less affluent. 3A was observed on four occasions by two different researchers. The following account draws on segments from three of these lessons.

Deirdre, 3A's teacher, always ensured students lined up quickly outside the classroom. She allowed six students at a time to enter to minimize fuss and disruption. Once inside, students stood behind their desks which were arranged in a horseshoe shape. After the morning greetings students then sat down and Deirdre began to call the roll as students sat quietly. This process was followed by a brief discussion of the previous night's homework and then the class was divided into two uneven groups. There was a small group of six students that included Eric and Walter who moved from their desks and sat on the floor to play a spelling game. The remaining students in the larger group, including Ben, were working from textbooks completing a series of spelling and vocabulary exercises. Deirdre had not provided any explanation in relation to these exercises. Students seemed to know what to do and simply opened their books and began working. Every now and then these students would murmur quietly or glance down at the students playing the game on the floor but generally this larger group was silent and very much engrossed in their work. The only real noise came from the group of students playing the spelling game on the floor, turning cards over in a 'concentration style' game to make words. Walter, Eric and the other four students were clearly having fun, as was Deirdre, but after 15 minutes she drew their attention to a series of spelling tasks she had written on the board for them to complete at their desks with the other students.

On making the move from the floor, however, both Walter and Eric appeared very distracted. They had difficulty settling down and lacked the drive and focus that Ben displayed who had been completing the textbook exercises and continued to do so with the same degree of concentration for a period of 40 minutes. Eric on the other hand spent a considerable amount of time fidgeting and playing with equipment on his desk doing very little work. Walter appeared to be daydreaming. In another lesson over a period of 45 minutes he was observed exhibiting similar behaviour quietly evading work – in fact not writing anything – despite Deirdre, who seemed a very attentive teacher, circulating around the room to check students' progress and offer advice. Deirdre had explained that both Walter and Eric had problems with their work but this was compounded by their difficulty concentrating. They may have enjoyed the activity they played on the floor but it seemed to have had an unsettling effect as they were then unable to assume the appropriate composure for engaging in literate practice; a composure that would have focused their attention to the task they were required to complete. This is not to say that they were not quiet, they were, but unproductively so. Their composure did not constitute a readiness to work, rather, it was indicative of an inability to do so. The larger group of students appeared to make a relatively seamless transition from the orderly nature of the beginning of the lesson to commencing their work. The smaller group's activity, however, had involved a form of comportment and communal engagement quite different to that which was required at their desks. For some students already disposed to scholarly endeavour such a move may not have presented a problem. For Eric and Walter, however, the staging of these activities had an unsettling effect and, without the appropriate scaffolding to focus their attention, were simply reliant on an existing habitus which was not inclined towards sustained concentration. They simply wasted much of the remainder of the lesson and failed to complete their work; something Deirdre explained was a common occurrence with both of these students, but especially Eric.

We characterize this as a discipline of control. Moreover, the lesson seemed to reinforce the dispositions students already possessed. The regime of silence and control that pervaded the classroom, especially when the smaller group had returned to their desks, was not really used in any productive way. It may have allowed the larger group of mostly Chinese students to concentrate on completing their textbook exercises, which seemed to replicate the kind of work offered in coaching colleges, but it afforded little opportunity for discussion and the development of the capacities of oral participation and critical thought around language that many of these students were said to lack. As Dooley (2003) discovered in her study of Chinese students in Australian schools, in some cases teachers' pedagogy was partly responsible for the docility and quiet that the Chinese students displayed and this seemed very much the case in Deirdre's classroom. This is not to say that the students were not encouraged to engage in discussion on other occasions and in fact an account of one such instance follows. The ease at which the students completed work in their textbooks and were able to do so for such a long period of time, however, suggests this was a regular practice and one that could have been varied to foster the skills Deirdre indicated many lacked.

On the following day in another afternoon lesson there was more of an emphasis on discussion. Students were initially at their desks completing maths activities on measuring mass from the previous day. Deirdre was attending to other work and writing instructions on the board. After 15 minutes of quiet in which Walter and Eric were once again very distracted and Ben focused on completing his work, Deirdre placed students in groups to discuss their findings on measuring mass prior to a report back to the whole class by each group leader. During this five minutes of discussion there seemed little mention of each person's results; it was more a general chatter with some of the students who hadn't finished continuing to complete their written work. Deirdre then provided a quick reminder of what each group leader was required to say and one at a time called them to the front to summarize their group's results. This proved very difficult for most students who needed constant prompting from Deirdre to complete their group report. After ten minutes, dissatisfied with their responses, Deirdre gave her own summary and then distributed some sheets with related exercises for the class to complete. Students returned to their desks and for the next 15 minutes the familiar quiet returned as they settled down to what seemed a regular pattern of initial teacher input and then completing worksheets or textbook exercises.

Class discussion and more protracted and detailed teacher explanation were limited in this classroom. While periods of independent study are an essential component of effective classroom practice they need to be preceded by the appropriate scaffolding of the tasks students are to complete if this time is to be used constructively (Hammond, 2001). Otherwise, they are simply completing exercises that could just as easily be undertaken as homework, especially by students like Ben who found this work relatively routine. Together with this, students like Walter and Eric need periods of independent work to be supported by activities that enhance their capacity for bodily control and mindful concentration. Without this, the kind of discipline of quiet and control experienced in this classroom simply had a disabling effect confirming their lack of academic engagement.

Yupeng – A discipline of engagement

In 3B, at Colinville PS, a different regimen was evident. Of a class of 32 students, eight were of Chinese background; the remaining students were a diverse mix of Anglo, Indian and different Northern European backgrounds plus one Pasifika student. While many students at the school were of a relatively high SES, there were those, such as Yupeng, who were not. His family had arrived from China only two years earlier and spoke very little English. His oral language skills, however, had improved dramatically since that time as had his written English. Considerable emphasis was placed on his school work at home and Yupeng tended to be quiet and focused in the classroom to the extent that Tom, his teacher, said he 'lacked personality'. Yupeng seemed the type of student who, given the classroom regimen described in the previous vignette would be considered a 'passive learner'. In Tom's class, however, there was a much stronger emphasis on structured class discussion and teacher explanation to accompany periods of independent work and, within this environment, Yupeng appeared to thrive. He remained quiet and focused when required but also actively participated in class discussion. This was the case during the four observation lessons, two of which are described here. These two lessons formed part of a unit of work related to Roald Dahl's *Charlie and the Chocolate Factory* that 3B was reading. Following a theme around sweets and cake – the link with the text – the first of these two lessons involved the class making cupcakes and the second using this activity to write a recipe, the type of procedural text the class was learning to write at the time.

In the first lesson conducted after lunch students forwarded in and sat at their desks. Tom's room was an unusual L shape. Desks were arranged in rows facing a board in the horizontal section of the L. Floor space with another board and a number of computers and resources were located in the vertical section of the L. Tom had written instructions on the board and asked for a volunteer to read them aloud to the class. Yupeng's hand immediately shot up and he proceeded to read from the board. Following this, students forwarded out of class once again to wash their hands and on their return group leaders were appointed. Each was assigned a separate area in which to make the cakes where all the necessary ingredients had been laid out in advance. In Yupeng's group each student had a turn of stirring and then placed the mixture in cake tins, with group members negotiating the process. During this time Tom and Jay, the ESL teacher working with the class, checked students' progress and, despite the potential chaos of 32 children completing such an activity in a confined space, they seemed quite orderly with one student from each group taking their cake tins to the staffroom oven where Tom was loading them to be cooked and the remaining students cleared up.

After 45 minutes working on this activity, Jay called students to attention on the floor and explained how they were to write a procedure on this activity the next day. She discussed the process and questioned students about the structure and grammar of instructional texts. This session was conducted as a guided class discussion with students seated on the floor. Yupeng, as before, was actively engaged, volunteering answers to most questions and Jay carefully scaffolding the text they would write by drawing on the activity the group had just completed. After 20 minutes of outlining the procedure, students were then instructed to forward to their desks and to read their copy of *Charlie and the Chocolate Factory* or other material in the time remaining prior to the bell. Although there was a bit of noise it was interesting how students were checking their peers' behaviour, some 'shooshing' to stop any chatter so they could read in quiet. Just prior to the bell Jay clapped to gain the attention of the class then students packed up and left for the day.

This lesson was continued in the mid-morning session of the next day. Students had spent part of the morning icing and decorating their cakes. Jay, who was once again seated on the chair, started to count and students quickly forwarded to the floor. Tom was at the back of the class and was team-teaching with Jay during the lesson. She proceeded to write a scaffold of the text on the board and questioned students about aspects of the text recapping on key points. Yupeng, sitting close to the front, was actively involved in answering questions on aspects of grammar. On completing the scaffold, which included writing the first two steps for the procedure as a class on the board, Jay asked students to return to their desks and to use this to write their own procedure. As the board was difficult to see from his seat, Yupeng picked up his book, went to the board and quickly copied down the outline. Four other students followed Yupeng's example and they also returned to their desks to write. The class was given 30 minutes to write their text. Yupeng and his classmates worked in a quiet attentive manner with most completing a draft prior to forwarding out to lunch, each taking one of the finished iced cupcakes that had been placed on a tray on their way.

This lesson with 3B was in sharp contrast to 3A's at Chestervale. A discipline of engagement seemed to pervade this room. Students were gaining a more sophisticated understanding of text and grammar through the careful scaffolding by the teacher. Both Jay and Tom used students' responses to their questions to do this. Their teacher-directed approach effectively engaged students in the process and the concrete and highly motivating cooking activity that preceded this heightened their understanding and willingness to be involved. This was a concrete activity that was appropriately pitched, eliciting a sophisticated treatment of language from students. This approach was particularly effective for Yupeng who, though clearly studious and work focused, needed support to engage in discussion. While questioning and discussion occurred in 3A with Ben, Eric and Walter, it was not sustained and discussion was left up to the students themselves. As such, it lacked direction and soon petered out. Students need support for effective oral participation, particularly those with a LBOTE and ESL learners. The whole class nature of the activity in Tom and Jay's class created a sense of corporate involvement that had considerable effect. There was still an appropriate level of control within the class but of a type that encouraged rather than stifled discussion.

Discipline within schools, we have been suggesting, is not simply about classroom management, nor about class reproduction. It is a force upon which learning is contingent that teachers can harness to instil self-discipline and promote capacities in their students. Without this enabling dimension discipline may simply reinforce existing dispositions which may be problematic, as was the case with Walter and Eric. With Yupeng, however, the opposite was evident. The discipline generated by the techniques utilized within his class not only promoted much needed skills of oral participation but provided the time, quiet and space to work independently and practise his written language skills.

Braydon and Tim – A discipline of disabling control

Braydon and Tim were in a boys-only years 3/4 composite class at Aston PS which comprised of mainly Anglo students with some from Pasifika and Aboriginal backgrounds. Braydon, who was discussed in Chapter 2, was of Anglo background, while Tim had a Pasifika/Māori background. The gender split with a parallel girls-only class was the school's attempt to minimize behaviour problems and lift student performance. The following account draws on one of three lessons that was observed which was devoted to handwriting followed by a creative writing exercise.

Braydon and Tim's classroom was quite large with two columns of three rows of desks directed towards a whiteboard at the front. Behind these desks at the back of the room was another whiteboard with space in front for floor activities. Braydon was seated at a desk at the back, while Tim was on the other side of the room at a front desk. While class monitors handed out handwriting books, Anita, their teacher, used an overhead projector, to display the day's date and a short saying for students to copy into their books. Anita pointed out that when they had finished they could continue practising single letters in the next page of their handwriting booklet. There was no demonstration or discussion of posture, grip and the particular directionality of the letters to be written. There was very little engagement with the class at all, simply an instruction to write and be quiet. The boys opened their books and started work. While the noise level in the class did rise at regular intervals, after reprimands from Anita the boys quietened down and overall they were well-behaved.

Sitting quite close to Braydon, we were interested to see how long it took him to settle down to work. He fiddled with his pencil case and sorted through pens and pencils. When he did finally commence writing the researcher noticed he was left-handed. As he was sitting at the last desk on the right-hand side of a row of desks, this made writing difficult. So as not to impinge upon his neighbour, Braydon shifted his book to the right-hand edge of his desk with his elbow directed towards the front of the room. Seated in such a way, writing was an uncomfortable process and Braydon seemed to procrastinate over completing his work. Tim, on the other side of the room, also displayed posture that was inappropriate for writing. He was hunched right over his book with his face close to the page. This was similarly not corrected but at least Tim seemed far more engaged than Braydon, completing his handwriting exercises in the time provided. The writing of the class overall varied considerably. Some boys had quite a good hand but more often than not their writing was overly large with poorly formed letters. A number of the students had no idea about correct directionality in forming letters which not only affects ease of writing when students start to use cursive script; it also inhibits their ability to focus on content. As discussed in Chapter 3, writing technology needs to become transparent so students can focus on *what* they are writing rather than *how*.

Anita progressed around the room on two occasions during the 50 minutes that were devoted to the lesson – the rest of the time she was at her desk or talking to a classroom assistant who had entered the room after the lesson had begun and sat at the back of the room most of the time providing little assistance. It seemed her role was to maintain quiet and order among students and to let the boys get on with their work. Yet, without direction and intervention to correct problems, they were not only habituating poor technique but, in the case of Braydon and others, a capacity for work avoidance reminiscent of that observed in 3A with Walter and Eric. There were students such as BJ of Pasifika background, who finished early, but with little self-direction was unable to use his time productively. He went over to a book and magazine rack to read but soon lost interest and began doodling on a piece of paper back at his desk. As he was quiet and seemingly occupied his lack of engagement went unnoticed. While a discipline of control appeared to govern this pedagogic space it proved disabling as it seemed to either foster disinterest or else mask the problems some students were experiencing with handwriting.

Similar problems emerged with the next activity in this morning session. Anita asked students to move to the floorspace and each sat up straight in rows to impress Anita who was seated on a chair in front of them. She read the boys a short poem called *Smiley*, asked them the meaning of a word and then distributed a sheet for them to draw a picture of the character described in the poem and to write a diary entry about him. The best picture was to be awarded ten raffle tickets, a technique used to reward good behaviour in the class. There was no further discussion about the poem, ideas for what students might draw or more importantly how to write a diary entry based on the poem which was an unusual choice of genre given its descriptive rather than episodic nature. Many students were clearly unsure about what to do but returned to their desks to commence work. Braydon once again procrastinated, playing with his pens and talking to the assistant. When he finally commenced working it was to draw the picture that appeared to bear very little relevance to the character described in the poem. During this time Anita progressed around the room but little guidance was given. When she spoke it was mainly to offer praise. There was a continual hum in the room that would rise in volume at intervals but this was always kept in check. Like Braydon, Tim focused on his illustration before writing. After 25 minutes when Anita indicated time was almost up and students would have a minute or so to check their work, it was only at this point that Braydon scribbled the following down on his sheet:

Smlly hed never steeps has femlly was get of him thay wer net out o him.

Tim was less hurried but all he had written was the following caption for his picture:

If I was this person I wold fel unlovd.

Students were then asked to return to the floor where a number were selected to show their illustrations and read out their work, one of whom was Braydon. While a couple of students had written up to a paragraph, none produced a diary entry. They were all mainly descriptions of the character. Some had difficulty reading their work, as did Braydon, who stumbled with his three poorly spelt and constructed sentences. Despite this, Anita responded with 'Good one – what a great picture.'

The function of these vignettes is not so much to evaluate classroom practice but to consider their ramifications in terms of our conceptual understanding of modes of discipline and their consequences for the development of dispositions to learning. The schools in the study with low-SES Anglo students and those of Pasifika backgrounds tended to perform below average on statewide literacy and numeracy tests. Braydon's and Tim's results typify this. Practices in the home, rather than just the macro-concepts of class and ethnicity, provide some explanation for this as they contribute to a form of embodiment unsuited to schooling and academic endeavour, in effect impeding cognitive development. Practices within the classroom, however, can prove equally inhibitory. Tim, and especially Braydon, had not only failed to acquire capacities of effective literate practice within this classroom but the poor habits they already possessed were reinforced through inaction on the teacher's part. Together with this, Braydon's procrastination over work was indicative of a lack of interest which had become so habituated it would be difficult for him to apply himself to improve these poor skills.

Lottie and Darren – Engaging in learning

In Lottie and Darren's years 3/4 composite class at Allerton PS with a similar demographic to 3C, a different set of classroom practices were evident. Both Lottie and Darren were of Pasifika background and, as with their school's overall student population, were of a low SES. 3D was observed on four occasions by two researchers. The following is an account of one of these lessons which was held during a mid-morning session. There were 28 students in the class with a higher number of LBOTE students than 3C some of whom were first phase ESL learners. The students sat in groups of four at seven sets of desks each with a clear view of the board. Scott, the teacher, began the lesson with 3D's regular spelling mastery test. Students all sat quietly waiting to begin. Scott read out the spelling words, included each in a sentence and then repeated the word as he moved around the room checking students were not copying. When the test was finished, students exchanged sheets with their neighbour to be marked. Scott chose students to spell each word before they were then handed back to him at the front to check. This was followed by a short dictation with Lottie, Darren and the rest of the class listening intently. On completing this, Scott provided immediate feedback choosing students to spell each content word. The class then proceeded to complete some related exercises in a textbook with Scott moving around to each student to check both this and the dictation. There was a bit of chatter but generally students were on-task. Darren finished quickly and sat up quietly with his arms folded on the desk. Shortly after this, Scott asked students to pass their books to the front.

These activities proved a suitable segue into the maths activity that followed. Students were asked to move to the floorspace at the front and Scott commenced a class discussion about graphs, referring initially to their previous day's work on the topic. He questioned students about the purpose of graphs and what was required in constructing their own, demonstrating what to do on the board. He went on to discuss different types of data that could be graphed based on students' interests. Students were quite engaged in the discussion and volunteered possible topics such as students' favourite pets, foods and colours. Both Lottie and Darren sat cross-legged close to the front and listened intently. Students were then asked to vote on a topic to research and most selected favourite pets. Categories were selected, for example, cats, dogs and rabbits, six in all and students indicated their preference by a show of hands. Scott felt that more 'data' was required and so a group of six students were sent next door to record the favourite pets of another Year 3 class. Meanwhile, the remaining students returned to their desks and organized their page to begin work. After two or three minutes, when the students returned with the data from the other class, Scott added their information to the board, tallied amounts and asked students to construct the axes for their graphs he had previously demonstrated in their books. Scott moved around the room checking students' work. Despite a small amount of chatter, most seemed very engaged. When this task was complete, Scott demonstrated how to record data on the graph, modelling the results for two types of pets and then having students complete the remainder. This process was then replicated with another topic – favourite foods – with students then asked comparative questions about the two graphs. Lottie had been working quietly on her own and offered responses to these. Darren, who tended to have a bit of a chat during this time, still completed his work and also showed an eagerness to respond to questions.

Not only was there a far greater degree of teacher direction and explanation in the class compared with 3C, there was also more student involvement. Scott seemed to keep students' behaviour in check through an appropriate staging of activities and maintaining a strong presence in the room. He also moved among students monitoring their progress during independent work and encouraging involvement during periods of whole class instruction. These techniques seemed to promote a discipline of engagement. This class was by no means made up of high-achieving or high-SES students, but something pedagogically significant was happening. Students were keen to be involved and, in doing so in such a focused and directed way, acquired important skills and understanding. The interest generated by the techniques Scott employed is crucial here. As Tomkins (1962, p. 33) explains, interest has a 'psychological function as an aid to sustained effort'. In effect, interest and ability operate in tandem and are central to the phenomenon we call *engagement*. It is the accumulation of interest that supplies the necessary effort to acquire ability. Interest and its accumulation, however, are not simply psychological; they have a bodily dimension as in the capacities acquired through effort. They constitute the dispositions to learning that are the focus here and, rather than specific to any particular ethnic group, are formed through the repeated engagement in practices that foster such dispositional tendencies.

Finau – Learning to be disengaged

The 28 students in Finau's class at Broughton Heights PS were from a range of backgrounds: Pasifika, Chinese, Anglo, Vietnamese, Lebanese and Iraqi with the first two being the largest groups. Most of these students, including Finau, were of a low SES and many were experiencing problems with both their oral and written English. Finau, of a Pasifika/Tongan background, was near the bottom in reading and maths and struggled with his school-work. His class was observed on four occasions by two researchers and this account is based on one of these. In this session students forwarded into class after a short, orderly morning assembly in the main quadrangle. Kate, Finau's teacher, had organized the desks in the classroom into four groups, two with boys and two with girls. Finau sat at the back of the room at a desk with his Pasifika mates, Fred and Eli, and a couple of Chinese and Arabic-speaking boys. The orderliness of the assembly dissipated very quickly on students entering the room. There was quite a bit of noise as students chattered, swung back and forth on their chairs and played with equipment on their desks, including soft toys and drink bottles that seemed to take pride of place. Over this clatter and talk Kate said 'Good Morning' but without gaining a suitable response she started to count to attract students' attention. Although this managed to quieten the class, silence was not maintained and there was a constant hum in the classroom that was at times checked by Kate with either more counting, reprimands or techniques such as 'hands-on-heads' or 'fingers-on-lips'. Amid this noise, Finau also swung on his chair and fiddled with his pencils. Unable to achieve quiet, Kate simply started the lesson which involved a discussion of the week's spelling words, a different list for different ability groups in the class followed by students copying their words into workbooks. Although students had no more than ten words to write, this activity took 30 minutes.

Students worked at various rates. Some finished early and settled down to read or complete other work but many were slow to start, Finau, Fred and Eli especially so. Instead, they were enjoying kicking each other under the table and attempting to disrupt other students in their group with various levels of success. Fred and Eli eventually commenced writing but Finau hadn't even put pen to paper when one of the other students at his table – a Chinese boy – had already finished and started reading.

During this time Kate moved around the room checking other students' work or having students come to her desk at the other side of the room directly opposite to where Finau was sitting. She did not seem aware of the different levels of application within the class. When Finau finally did get down to work and finish he then left the class to put something in his bag and when he returned he roamed around the room at one point playing with a toy clock on a cupboard at the back. Finally, he was asked to sit down as the class moved onto one of two language-related activities, both included a short period of discussion in which students showed limited interest. Finau and Eli demonstrated great difficulty with the writing and Kate assisted them out the front and then had them copy out what they had undertaken together. This, however, also proved difficult for the boys. They were frequently distracted by others at their group of desks and had difficulty concentrating, though by this stage the task they were required to complete lacked any intellectual rigour, it was simply copying – busy work. This was very much the type of work the class as a whole undertook, what seemed like a series of unrelated tasks without sustained treatment of a topic and the appropriate scaffolding.

As a result, a discipline of disengagement governed this pedagogic space which was not simply a function of Kate's poor curriculum implementation; it was also generated by the regimen of restlessness that pervaded the room. While Walter, Eric and Braydon from some of the other classrooms that were observed, also displayed disengaged behaviour it seemed a function of a different type of disciplinarity, namely a discipline of control that proved disabling for these students. Quiet was enforced but indifference continued as students appeared to have little interest to propel them. With Finau the situation was quite different. The class evoked a discipline that was disengaging that didn't even afford the possibility for concentration through an enforced quiet and control. Some students with an existing habitus inclined towards academic endeavour may have been able to apply themselves to their work, and indeed this seemed to be the case. For many, such as Finau, the techniques employed in this classroom failed to equip them with the discipline to learn and, left to rely on their existing habitus, they simply floundered and instead appeared to be cultivating a disposition of indifference towards their schoolwork.

Vincent – Enabling control and productive quietness

Vincent, a student of Chinese background, was in a 3/4 composite class across the hall from Finau at Broughton Heights PS. As he had arrived late in the year from another school he was placed in the only class with a vacancy. His teacher, Carly, referred to it as 'the strangest class I've ever had'. Composite classes are generally comprised of a number of independent workers given the teacher is required to direct their attention to different groups at different times of the day, yet Carly's class had very few really able children. As it was 90 per cent LBOTE, with mainly Arabic-speaking, Chinese and Pasifika students, there were a number who required ESL support including two Afghani refugees and two African refugees.[1] There were also two deaf children and two students with a mild intellectual disability (MID) who had been integrated into this mainstream class. They were a handful to say the least and so Carly was very strict in relation to discipline.

This lesson was one of three observation sessions. It occurred halfway through the middle session of the day when students tend to get a bit restless yet the Year 4 students were sitting at their desks in a group arrangement, quiet and focused. Carly was sitting on the floor with the Year 3 students discussing a comprehension exercise they were about to complete. Questions were written on a board close by and Carly was discussing each with the students and possible answers. She insisted that students replied with full sentences and demonstrated how to do this using part of the question. Sitting in a circle on the floor students seemed excited and engaged in the lesson but Carly insisted they sit correctly and didn't call out, though she did encourage quite a bit of orderly discussion. When she felt satisfied that they understood what was required, the students moved to their desks to complete the activity. With the exception of one of the MID children, who was distracted but not disturbing others, students settled down quickly to work. Activities seemed fast-paced. After ten minutes of sustained work students returned to the floor to discuss their work with Carly who then collected books to be marked.

This activity was followed by a Maths lesson. Using plastic blocks Carly engaged the class in a concrete activity about fractions on the floor before moving onto an abstract treatment of the same process using textbook examples with numerical notation. She discussed a number of these and then had those children who felt confident return to their desks to complete a set of equations. The remainder stayed with Carly on the floor and she gave these students some further explanation about the transition from the concrete to the abstract formulation. Vincent was one of those who moved to his desk. He quickly completed his work, had Carly check each answer and then moved to one of the two computers in the room to complete extension maths work. Some other children who finished their work went on to read books prior to lunch.

While there were various sites of learning in this classroom most children appeared engaged in their particular activity. The capacities these students demonstrated, such as an application to work, seemed to have a direct relationship to the pedagogy that Carly employed. No doubt, as a function of practices within his home, Vincent clearly possessed a habitus that inclined him to academic endeavour, yet this may not have been the case with other students such as the Pasifika children and the Afghanis and Africans, the latter with disrupted schooling. It appears that over a period of time in Carly's class these students had embodied the skills required for independent work. While the disciplinary force generated by Carly's pedagogy tended towards control, it also had an enabling effect, unlike that found in Eric, Walter and Braydon's classrooms. This was not a class where constant docility was the rule. Their stillness and quiet was by-and-large productive. This class was capable of sustained concentration and application and, if needed, discussion. Carly balanced control with engagement through her discussion and scaffolding of her students' learning, and, in the process, encouraged capacities of a scholarly nature.

Disciplinary modes and dispositions to learning

Bloomer and Hodkinson (2000) argue that despite the substantial research on classroom learning, little of this has focused on the ways that students' dispositions to learning change. Our ethnographies of classroom practice make a contribution towards filling this gap. While 70 observation sessions were conducted in 18 classrooms, these six vignettes broadly represent the practices exhibited overall showing the differences in organization, classroom management and curriculum implementation, each of which was indicative of a particular disciplinary mode that had a marked impact on students' dispositions to learning, regardless of their ethnic background. In some classes with less effective teachers there was evidence of either a disabling discipline of control or one of disengagement. The former was characterized by a pedagogy of minimal teacher input, ineffectual supervision and yet maximum quiet and control. Such an approach appeared to do little more than replicate each student's existing habitus for learning. In the case of students like Ben, who was of Chinese background, this was not necessarily a problem, yet it provided only limited opportunities for engagement in class discussion and critical thought. For other students, without a disposition for academic endeavour, pedagogies such as these proved disabling as their lack of engagement was never satisfactorily addressed, impacting on their overall skill development and acquisition of knowledge. A similar effect was apparent in classrooms where a discipline of disengagement appeared the norm. Although, without adequate quiet and control, these classrooms were even more problematic as even those students with a greater degree of self-discipline could be easily distracted, affecting concentration and the quality of their work.

There were classrooms, however, where practices prevailed that augmented students' existing capabilities. In each of these there was both a strong teacher presence and active student participation effectively scaffolded by the teacher. These classrooms were characterized by different modes of discipline; either a discipline of control that proved enabling or a discipline of engagement. The former was evident in Vincent's classroom and, while not apparent in his case, most students in his class lacked the necessary self-discipline to apply themselves to their work for sustained periods. The techniques that Carly, his teacher, employed, while tending towards a discipline of control, appeared effective in promoting students' engagement in learning. She had established routines in the class to regulate student behaviour such as limited, or no, talk during periods of independent work and strict rules regarding movement and use of equipment. This was matched by a highly scaffolded approach to curriculum delivery resulting in effective student participation. Vincent appeared to excel in this class due to a high degree of congruence between these disciplinary practices and those within his home. For other students without this advantage the routines they met in the classroom were clearly encouraging a greater engagement in learning though persistent intervention of this type would be necessary for these students to acquire a disposition more inclined towards scholarly pursuits.

In Yupeng, Lottie and Darren's classrooms the level of control may not have been so intense yet there were measures in place to effectively regulate student behaviour to promote engagement in learning. These took the form of a highly scaffolded approach to curriculum delivery, considerable teacher explanation and close monitoring of student progress during lessons. The latter was more apparent in Lottie's and Darren's classroom as students were experiencing greater difficulties with their learning and lacked the same degree of self-discipline that Yupeng and most of his classmates displayed. As such, checks for on-task behaviour were required far more regularly. These two classrooms seemed to exhibit a discipline of engagement and while students in 3B appeared more disposed to academic endeavour, this approach also proved enabling for 3D.

This chapter indicates that we not only need to provide detailed ethnographies of classrooms and schools to offer telling insights into how students' capacities are formed, but that we need to develop a more conceptually profound framework for thinking through the role of disciplinary regimens in fostering scholarly dispositions to learning. Despite the differences in ethnicity, socio-economic background and gender of the students in the study, it seemed there were certain classroom practices that were effective for all students in promoting a disposition to learning. These practices typically included: effective scaffolding of curriculum, both in terms of content and the language students required to process it, detailed teacher explanation and active student participation. Together with this, it appeared students required both quiet and time for independent application of knowledge and skills, yet with the appropriate support and supervision of teachers if required. In classrooms where these practices were evident students seemed to thrive no matter what their ethnic background. This is not to say that ethnicity and cultural identity are of little importance in terms of schooling, but it is important to bear Holliday's comment in mind that, 'If we think of a people's behaviour as defined and constrained by the culture in which they live, agency is transferred away from the individual to the culture itself' (Holliday, 2005, p. 18). The students of Chinese, Pasifika and Anglo backgrounds investigated in this study all had the potential to succeed academically, yet it was the practices they engaged in at home and school that either assisted or impeded this process. While it may be difficult to alter long standing practices within the home, schools have a huge responsibility to ensure classroom practices effectively meet students' needs and appropriately augment the capacities embodied within the home ensuring each develops the necessary dispositions to learn and succeed at school.

Conclusion

Ethnicity, or a matter of practice

This book has sought to examine the links between ethnicity and what we have termed the *scholarly habitus*, the dispositions to learning that are essential for successful participation in schooling. By showing the tendencies of Chinese students to perform exceptionally well at school compared to the relatively poor performance of many from Pasifika backgrounds it could be argued that we have simply reinforced the stereotypical representations of these students that are prevalent in the media. Yet rather than presenting their educational achievement as an automatic consequence of ethnicity, we have instead examined the practices these students are engaged in, both inside and outside school, to gauge the extent to which these are formative in their differential achievement. These practices are, of course, patterned by ethnicity together with class, gender and a range of other factors but, by using practice as the starting point, we feel we have been able to more effectively investigate the basis of these stereotypes and to understand the ways in which certain educational capacities are acquired.

Despite the complex and constructed nature of ethnicity as a category, it is all too readily used as a way of explaining the differential educational achievement of students from non-Anglo backgrounds. While this study was not investigating students' ethnic identity as such, it became clear that being 'Chinese', 'Pasifika' or 'Anglo' was experienced very differently by individual students. Many who considered themselves of Chinese background had arrived in Australia from China, Hong Kong, Singapore or Malaysia. Others were Australian-born and their families had been living in Australia for a number of years. Those termed 'Pasifika' had similarly varied backgrounds especially given this label is simply a term of convenience used to refer to students from a wide range of Pacific nations with very different languages, traditions and histories. The label 'Anglo', however, posed other problems given it tended to operate as an ethnically neutral term by teachers, who either saw students of Anglo background as individuals or privileged categories such as class or gender in explaining these students' academic performance. To complicate matters further, there were some students who actually had quite mixed cultural heritages. Fred, one of the Pasifika students whose family had migrated from Fiji, had a grandparent who was Chinese.

Given this complexity one could ask why use the terms 'Chinese', Pasifika' or 'Anglo' in the first place or indeed bother to examine the relationship between ethnicity and academic performance if these ethnic categories are so contingent. In terms of both social perceptions and forms of self-identification, however, these categories are meaningful for people and therefore are useful as a necessary starting point for analysis. Because ethnicity is a socially and historically constructed category, not despite this, it is a useful tool for exploring the social patterns of commonality and difference in practices and outcomes. The fact that ethnicity is so vexed should not inhibit its use as an initial category of analysis; it just means we need to be judicious about the way in which we assign coherence to ethnic group membership and how we use it to make sense of empirical data.

As Brubaker (2004) points out, groupness based on ethnicity is an accomplishment in specific circumstances based on a heterogeneous mix of factors constitutive of identity, not an inevitable consequence of ancestry. By foregrounding practice, rather than ethnicity, it meant we were able to place emphasis on the capacities required for effective academic performance, how these are acquired and how they are distributed. This shift in focus does not reduce achievement to a product of individual performance, downplaying the impact of sociocultural processes; rather it allows for a more nuanced analysis of students' cultural background. In such a way culture is not simply perceived as ethnicity, or even a more sophisticated construct involving class and gender but, as Wicker (1997, p. 40) explains, 'as a set of dispositions acquired by individuals in the process of living'. Educational achievement, therefore, should not only be viewed as a product of these macro-social processes but what students do in the course of their everyday lives and their acquisition of certain dispositions to learning.

Embodied dispositions to learning

The students that we investigated from across these three groups often appeared to have quite differently capacitated bodies. As we observed them in classrooms, we saw some who displayed a readiness to work. They were quiet and still, sat upright and listened attentively. If they were required to work independently they settled quickly showing concentration and a sustained application to work. They also seemed to have embodied a particular posture for literate practice. They had assumed a naturalness about the grip of their pen, ease with writing and a certain orientation that Munns (2007) refers to as 'in-task' as opposed to just 'on-task' behaviour. They were engaged in learning but this seemed predicated on their bodily capacity to do so, a discipline to learn that governed their approach to scholarly endeavour. The form of composure and focused attention they displayed to independent work did not seem to inhibit these children from also actively participating in class discussion and group activities. These observable cognitive abilities were not simply a function of psychological predisposition but were more a matter of embodied habits that had become almost automatic; acquired tendencies formed through repeated and calibrated performance. They can be considered *second nature* in that they seem 'natural' but are actually 'cultural'. Yet because they are the product of innumerable, accumulated and routinized everyday practices they are often mistaken as naturally occurring or pathologized as a behavioural characteristic of particular ethnic groups.

While we sat in classrooms and observed students who displayed these capacities, there were others who did not. Rather than being disposed to learn, there were many who exhibited little bodily control and lacked any real engagement in learning. They were restless and fidgeted; played with equipment on their desks, rocked back and forth on their chairs and chatted unproductively to other students. They had great difficulty applying themselves to their work and displayed an awkwardness towards writing often evident in their slumped posture and poor pen grip. These students had habituated a disengagement that did not dispose them to scholarly activity. Without the appropriate degree of self-regulation neither their bodies nor their minds were focused on learning. They had simply not acquired the necessary embodied dispositions for successful participation in schooling.

Still other students exhibited quite different forms of embodiment. There were those who were quiet during independent work but unproductively so. They had developed capacities for task avoidance remaining quiet to avoid detection by teachers but lacking the discipline to apply themselves to their work in any sustained way. They exhibited a kind of disengagement which, while not disruptive, was nevertheless disabling. Generally these students had difficulty with writing, not only in terms of style and content but the mechanical process of forming letters which was impacting upon their progress. Quiet, as with talk, showed itself to be both productive and unproductive.

While there were students from across the three groups who had embodied these different dispositions towards learning, there was a strong tendency for those of Chinese background to display the capacities which seemed to dispose them more towards scholarly engagement. Sonia, discussed in

Chapter 3, seemed to typify this. There were far more Anglo and Pasifika students in the classrooms whose behaviour marked them as disengaged. They were either noisy and restless, like Sonny, or unproductively quiet and lacking application, like Eric. This disparity in embodied capital seemed to align with the different aspirations the parents and students from across the three groups held. The Chinese parents seemed to have much higher aspirations for their children, especially in relation to them attending a selective high school or with their future careers. Their children were also far more likely to nominate a professional occupation rather than a manual or service job than were the Anglo or Pasifika students. While differences in SES seemed to impact on the choices of the Anglo and Pasifika students this was less likely the case with those of Chinese background. These students seemed to have a keen desire to achieve no matter what their SES with this desire assuming a material form as bodily capacity. These students were not simply driven as a function of what some simply refer to as 'ethnic drive'; rather, their desire to achieve seemed to fuel and to be fuelled by this bodily capacitation.

This patterning of different dispositions to learning across the three groups was interpreted in various ways by the teachers drawing on what we have called multicultural schemas of perception. While many were keen to avoid the stereotypes of Chinese and Pasifika learners, their inability to reflect in depth on questions of pedagogy and to grapple with 'culture' in anything but reductive terms, meant that they were not able to offer any suitable explanation for these patterns without recourse to these stereotypes. Rather than achievement being viewed as an outcome of practices, to many teachers it was simply an attribute of culture, perceived in terms of ethnicity.

Home, school and the formation of a scholarly habitus

An examination of the practices students engaged in both at home and school, however, revealed considerable differences between the three groups. The Chinese students not only spent more time on their homework and completed more of it; the routinized nature of what they did, organized through temporal and spatial practices and parental supervision,was also significant. While some teachers were critical of what they saw as an overemphasis on homework by many Chinese parents, this regularity is important to the formation of habits. With Dewey, we would argue that habits of learning are the consequence of particular and productive forms of routine and repetition (Watkins, 2011b). Through regular completion of homework many of the Chinese students were developing a discipline towards independent study; a second nature ingrained though practice. In effect they were receiving a kind of academic apprenticeship, a training of the body for scholarly endeavour.

This instilling of a particular self-control and discipline within many of the Chinese students was also fostered by a high level of involvement in extracurricular pursuits. While SES seemed to play a role in limiting the activities some Anglo and Pasifika students participated in, it did not appear to inhibit the participation of the Chinese students. Many of the Pasifika students, on the other hand, engaged in very few extracurricular pursuits. This was especially the case with the girls. While many attended church-related dancing and singing activities that had a strong social focus, there did not seem the same imperative to learn a skill or for their time to be occupied with more structured activities outside school. Chinese and high-SES Anglo students tended to read far more in their own time than the Pasifika and low-SES Anglo students. Overall, however, it was the Chinese students who used local libraries more regularly than other students. Reading and literary culture appeared to be highly prized, but not simply as an aesthetic taste. Rather, value here assumed a materiality inscribed in students' bodies as productive habits formed through iterative performance.

These different emphases on academic pursuits outside school had considerable bearing on how students approached their work at school. Together with this, the pedagogic practices of their teachers seemed to either reinforce the students' existing habitus or, was able to encourage new and productive habits of learning. A range of practices engendering differing degrees or modalities of discipline were evident across the six schools. These modalities of discipline appeared to function in four distinct ways, as: a disabling discipline of control; an enabling discipline of control; a discipline of disengagement or; a discipline of engagement.

The notion of discipline used here does not simply pertain to control operating as a negative force inhibiting learning. While a disabling discipline of control was apparent in the pedagogy some teachers employed and also framed some of the whole school practices, there were forms of discipline that proved enabling, capacitating students' bodies and promoting effective habits of learning. Discipline in this sense appeared to be much in line with Foucault's view that, 'a disciplined body is the prerequisite of an efficient gesture' (1977, p. 152). It is a discipline that predisposes students towards particular types of endeavour; taking the form of dispositions within the habitus. Differing degrees of discipline resulting from the repeated performance of certain practices distinguishes successful and unsuccessful students. Although there was some variation, there were patterns across the three ethnically defined groups in this study. However, for all students where positive forms of discipline were generated, such as an enabling discipline of control and a discipline of engagement, active participation in learning and sustained application resulted. These forms of discipline generated by teachers' pedagogic practice proved enabling for all students in the classrooms where they were evident, regardless of the students' ethnicity. For many of the Chinese students, however, this was particularly the case because they had already embodied a discipline to learn from routines established within the home. The relative congruence between home and school supported their learning. In classrooms where negative forms of discipline were the norm, such as a disabling discipline of control and a discipline of disengagement, students were less likely to be actively engaged in learning. Many, especially those from Pasifika or low-SES Anglo backgrounds, were left to rely on their existing habitus to provide the motor or discipline to learn. There were too many distractions for those students who lacked the self-discipline to participate effectively and school reinforced their unproductive habits. In classrooms characterized by a disabling discipline of control, a different dynamic was evident, yet with similar effect.

Lessons learnt

This study contributes to contemporary debates primarily through its attempt to reorientate Bourdieu's notion of habitus away from the dominant emphasis on its role in the reproduction of relations of power to one which draws on the generative nature of the habitus. It is imperative that educational researchers follow an increasing number of social theorists who have developed a more nuanced conceptualization which recognizes the transformative potential in Bourdieu's theoretical framework which suggests possibilities for schools and teachers to improve the educational outcomes of all students (Mills, 2008). Extending and elaborating the notions of disposition and discipline, by making them connect to detailed ethnographies of classrooms, is a crucial step in this process. So too is the theoretical focus on social practices. The significance of this focus is twofold: it allows us to think more intricately about how human capacities are acquired, and it allows us to think about how and why we might change them. These are both of enormous consequence in analysing the relation between ethnicity and education, for they allow us to step away from the tendency in popular, professional and academic discourse to essentialize and pathologize educational outcomes. It means not ignoring the exceptions, and it means thinking about how skills are acquired and developed.

Yet this also requires that we think seriously about the goals and methods of educational research and teaching practice. What is the purpose of educational research? To read much of what passes as critical scholarship, it is to rediscover over and over the inequalities that shape educational outcomes. What if we shifted that to a focus on the capacities that schooling produces, the capacities that students need in the worlds they live in, and how these capacities are learnt and distributed? As we have suggested in this book, too often the focus on schooling as a form of reproduction is translated to mean that all its valued skills and knowledges are forms of class reproduction. Our view is that many of these are skills and knowledges which are monopolized by the powerful, and the work of educational reform is to redistribute them, to make them available to be appropriated by the disadvantaged. A focus on teaching and learning practice as the acquisition of capacities means we can legitimately ask how we can do this task better.

For some researchers and practitioners, this poses a problem, because the culture of schooling is seen to be antagonistic to the 'authentic' cultures of the marginalized, and teaching becomes, in Bourdieu and Passeron's (1990) overused phrase, 'symbolic violence', or the imposition by the powerful upon the powerless in ways of thinking and acting as a form of domination. If this means teaching English to refugee students, numeracy to low SES students or critical analysis to all students, then the only solution is to dismantle all systems of education. One strand of scholarship, for example, critiques the very idea of the 'good student' as a discursive construct designed to perpetuate normative, white, middle-class ideals of conduct (Grant, 1997; McLeod and Yates, 2006, p. 50). There is a truth in this, of course, but the problem with this argument is that it throws the educational baby out with the bath water. If we recognize what Bourdieu seems to dismiss as the 'technical' dimensions of intellectual knowledge and skills as part of the 'educational necessary' (Nash, 2002a) then we have to have a more robust discussion about what schools *should* teach.

Nash takes issue with this implication of Bourdieu's work. He found that progress at school is associated with, alongside non-cognitive dispositions around aspiration and academic self-concept, a willingness to be subjected to the pedagogic and disciplinary order of schooling. Nash's study specifically included working-class students with 'average ability'. Yet, rather than critique this as demonstrating class domination, Nash argues that if a school 'is to respond to habitus that generate practices that result in failure rather than success, then it can do so only by an intensification of its power as an agency of socialisation' (2002b, p. 36). We would add to this that the capacities that schooling provides do not have to devalue or remove the cultural values that students bring with them – they may challenge them, but if learning is about the accumulation of capacities, then schooling is a process of augmentation, not necessarily erasure.

It also means that we need to think about not just the goals of education generally, but the goals of multicultural education. If the well-intentioned efforts of teachers in addressing the needs of marginalized ethnic groups reproduce stereotypical perceptions of those students and result in programmes that reproduce disadvantage, then they need to be urgently reconsidered. Given the prevalence of ethnicized schemas of perception among teachers, however, we aren't just talking about removing or refocusing these programmes; we need professional learning experiences for teachers that provide the wherewithal to deconstruct their professional vision and to implement programmes that engage substantially with the cultural complexity of their students.

As researchers, we might want to consider the consequences of this in two key ways. We might want to reflect upon our relationship to teaching practice, and whether we can provide the kind of professional learning we have just described in ways that don't simply tell teachers they are instruments of social reproduction. We might also want to consider how an analysis of education might change our understandings of ethnicity. If the logical conclusion of the argument that ethnicities are things constructed through diverse practices in relation to social contexts, then what role does education have, not just in realizing the aspirations of ethnically defined groups, but in fashioning an ethnic identity itself? As Du (2010, p. 6) and Louie (2004) suggest, education is a key site through which Chinese Americans develop an ethos that responds to the conditions they find themselves in, and which generates practices and dispositions that articulates with the racial order.

Lastly, we want to stress again the productive nature of habit and its role in the bodily dimensions of learning, which are given little emphasis within contemporary pedagogy (Watkins, 2011b). Skills of self-discipline and sustained application to work are not only configured as natural abilities but are seen to be of little relevance in the early years of school, even anathema to the dominant ethos of learning through play. The fact that such skills have to be developed early on to contribute to successful participation at school is simply overlooked. While it is important for parents to encourage effective habits of learning within the home, as was the case with many of the Chinese and other parents in this study, this is not enough. Schools and systems do not only need to rethink their support of parents around these bodily aspects of children's learning but to focus on the school itself as an important site of intervention in this regard. There needs to be a greater awareness of the enabling potential of discipline and for schools to promote practices that allow *all* students to develop the capacities of a scholarly habitus on which successful performance at school depends.

Notes

Introduction

1 As this book suggests, such broad categories are problematic. Asia refers to the land mass that stretches from Turkey to the Pacific Ocean and from the Indian Ocean to the Arctic Ocean. Given this, it is primarily a cultural idea based on the geopolitical global order arising from European colonization rather than a coherent entity. Despite this, 'Asian' is often used as though it has an ethnic or racial coherence, though the perception of that coherence varies. In Australia, for example, 'Asian' refers to peoples of East Asian origin, that is, Chinese, Vietnamese, etc. and this is the usage employed in this book. In the United Kingdom, 'Asian' refers to peoples of sub-continental background, that is, Indian, Pakistani, Bangladeshi. 'Pasifika' is a term used to refer collectively to Polynesian peoples of Samoan, Tongan, Cook Islander, Māori, Fijian or Tokelauan backgrounds. It is preferred over 'Pacific Islander' in the case of Māori who, while of Polynesian background, see themselves as the indigenous people of New Zealand and not Pacific Islanders. This term was also favoured by the NSW Department of Education and Training with whom we collaborated on the Australian Research Council Project, *Discipline and Diversity: Cultural Practices and Learning* on which this book is based. The use of this category is not intended to homogenize the cultural diversity within this 'group' but merely to allow for ease of reference.

2 While we make some reference to the ways in which gender impacts upon the different practices the students engaged in, this was not a focus of the study. We acknowledge the work of Dumais (2002) and Reay (1995) who have more extensively examined the consequences of gender and schooling in the formation of the habitus.

3 Since 2008 all Australian school students have undertaken the National Assessment Program – Literacy and Numeracy or NAPLAN in Years 3, 5, 7 and 9. The test data in this study was collected from the 2006 NSW Basic Skills Test, a precursor to the NAPLAN.

4 The delineation as either middle/high or low SES is based on survey returns of parents' income and occupation and a serves only as a general categorization of SES.

5 Pseudonyms have been used in all cases. Pseudonyms have also been used for teachers, parents and community representatives but these are not listed in Table 0.1. Where relevant, participants' association with a school or student is indicated at that point.

6 The selection of schools chosen for inclusion in the second phase of the study was based on the return rate of surveys within the school, return rate of target groups within the school; and the level of interest demonstrated by school staff.

Chapter 1

1 L. Lu (2010), Inclusion of a LBOTE related measure in the school SES construct. *Culture, Language and Learning Forum*, NSW Department of Education and Training, 27 October.

2 Based on the 2006 census data for the two local government areas in which Epping is located, the dominant overseas country of birth in the suburb was China, representing 9.3 per cent of the local population, followed by Hong Kong with 6.1 per cent, both of which are substantially higher than the respective percentages for the Sydney Statistical Division (2.7% and 0.9%). Other Asian nations – Korea, India, Malaysia, Sri Lanka and Taiwan – also feature in the top ten countries of birth (Hornsby Shire Council, 2012; Parramatta City Council, 2012). These figures, of course, do not include the children of Chinese-born migrants.

3 Māori settled in New Zealand from Polynesia in the 1300s. White settlers began to arrive from the late eighteenth century and in 1840 the British Crown and Māori chiefs signed the Treaty of Waitangi. This brought New Zealand into the British Empire giving Māori equal rights with British citizens.

Chapter 2

1 We acknowledge the importance of also considering the ways ethnicity links with social capital – Bourdieu's concept to capture the significance of social networks in facilitating social life, as explored in the work of Modood (2004) and Shah et al. (2010).

2 On average, Australians earned $A42,081 in wages and salaries in 2006–7 (ABS, 2007).

3 It should be pointed out that there is no comparable social anguish about the long hours some children put into sports and music practice – or even community languages – outside normal school hours.

Chapter 3

1 The enrichment class was a selective class run in Years 3–6 at the school. The students were selected both on the basis of academic achievement and on the basis of a writing task where they indicated why they would like to be part of the class. Membership of the class was reconsidered each year.

2 There are, of course, a range of capacities that are productive in other actions. The physicality demonstrated by Sonny, for example, might be useful on a football field, where stillness and quiet are less valuable. But our point here is that educational achievement fundamentally requires the dispositions of the scholarly habitus.

3 The UNSW tests are run by a testing centre at the University of NSW, and schools can choose to opt into these tests, for a fee. OCs are specialist Years 5/6 classes that are located in specific schools and aim at catering for gifted and talented children, assessed by an optional exam in Year 4.

Chapter 4

1 This is not to neglect the important work within sociolinguistics such as that of Shirley Brice Heath (1983) and Ruqaiya Hasan (2009) exploring the differing literacy and linguistic practices across families of differing SES.

Chapter 6

1 Neither the ethnic background nor national origin of these students was disclosed and so they are simply referred to here as African.

References

Abboud, K. and Kim, J. (2005), *Top of the Class: How Asian Parents Raise High Achievers and How You Can Too*. New York: Berkeley Publishing Group.

Ahmed, S. (2004), Declarations of whiteness: the non-performativity of anti-racism. *Borderlands e-journal*, 3(2), <www.borderlandsejournal.adelaide.edu.au/vol3no2_2004/ahmed_declarations.htm>.

Allan, R. and Hill, B. (2004), Multicultural education in Australia: historical development and current status. In J. Banks and C. McGee Banks (eds), *Handbook on Research on Multicultural Education*. San Francisco: Jossey-Bass, 979–96.

Andres, L. (2009), The cumulative impact of capital on dispositions across time: a 15 year perspective of young Canadians. In K. Robson and C. Sanders (eds), *Quantifying Theory: Pierre Bourdieu*. New York: Springer, 75–88.

Anderson, C. and Bruce, C. (2004), Using family background to predict educational attainment in Canada. *Economica*, 9(3), <www.economica.ca/ew093p1.htm>.

Ang, I. (2001), *On Not Speaking Chinese: Living between Asia and the West*. Routledge: London.

— (2005), Who needs cultural research? In P. Leistyna (ed.),*Cultural Studies from Theory to Action*. Carlton, Victoria: Blackwell Publishing, 477–83.

Anonymous (2008), Let's not leave any child behind, *The New Zealand Herald*, 20 November, p. 11.

Archer, L. (2008), The impossibility of minority ethnic educational 'success'? An examination of the discourses of teachers and pupils in British secondary schools. *European Educational Researcher Journal*, 7(1), 89–107.

Archer, L. and Francis, B. (2006), Challenging classes? Exploring the role of social class within the identities and achievement of British Chinese pupils. *Sociology*, 40(1), 29–49.

Atkinson, W. (2011), From sociological fictions to social fictions: some Bourdieusian reflections on the concepts of 'institutional habitus' and 'family habitus'. *British Journal of Sociology of Education*, 32(3), 331–47.

Au, K. H. and Kawakami, A. J. (1994), Cultural congruence in instruction. In E. R. Hollins, W. C. Hayman and J. E. King (eds), *Teaching Diverse Populations: Formulating a Knowledge Base*. New York: SUNY Press, 5–23.

Australian Associated Press (AAP) (2002), Ethnicity, school factors in university success. *AAP Newsfeed*, 18 January.

Australian Bureau of Statistics (2007), 2001 Population census – occupation groups, labour force status, qualifications and family income for persons of Chinese, Polynesian and English-speaking backgrounds. ABS, Canberra.

— (2011), 6 million migrants call Australia home, <www.abs.gov.au/ausstats/abs@.nsf/Latestproducts/3412.0Media%20Release12009–0?opendocumentandtabname= Summaryandprodno=3412.0andissue=2009–10andnum=andview=>.

Australian Council of State School Organisations (ACSSO) (2007), *Homework: Hot Topic*, editorial, <www.acsso.org.au/AED070410.pdf>.

Australian Government (2011), *The People of Australia: Australia's Multicultural Policy*. Canberra: Department of Immigration and Citizenship, <www.immi. gov.au/media/publications/multicultural/pdf_doc/people-of-australia-multicult ural-policy-booklet.pdf>.

Baird, J. (2011), Applaud children who kick all goals. *Sydney Morning Herald*, 28 January, p. 11.

Barnard, W. M. (2004), Parent involvement in elementary school and educational attainment, *Children and Youth Services Review*, 26, 39–62.

Bartock, D. (2009), Police tackle Islander Gangs, Parramatta Advertiser, 10 September, <http://parramatta-advertiser.whereilive.com.au/news/story/ police-tackle-islander-gangs/>.

Besley, T. and Peters, M. (2007), *Subjectivity and Truth: Foucault, Education, and the Culture of Self*. New York: Peter Lang.

Biggs, J. (1996), Western misconceptions of the Confucian-heritage learning culture. In D. A. Watkins and J. B. Biggs (eds), *The Chinese Learner: Cultural Psychological and Contextual Influences*. Melbourne: ACER, 45–67.

Birrell, B. (1987), The educational achievement of non-English speaking background students. In L. Baker and P. Miller (eds), *The Economics of Immigration*. Canberra: Department of Industry, Local Government and Ethnic Affairs, 91–121.

Blackledge, A. (2001), The wrong sort of capital? Bangladeshi women and their children's schooling in Birmingham, UK. *International Journal of Bilingualism*, 5(3), 345–69.

Bloomer, M. and Hodkinson, P. (2000), Learning careers: continuity and change in young people's dispositions to learning. *British Educational Research Journal*, 26(5), 583–97.

Bodovski, K. (2010), Parental practices and educational achievement: Social class, race, and habitus. *British Journal of Sociology of Education*, 31(2), 139–56.

Boggiano, A. and Pittman, T. (eds) (1992), *Achievement and Motivation*. Cambridge: Cambridge University Press.

Bottomley, G. (1979), *After the Odyssey*. St Lucia: University of Queensland Press.

Bourdieu, P. (1984), *Distinction*, trans. R. Nice. Cambridge, MA: Harvard University Press.

— (1986), The three forms of capital. In J. Richardson (ed.), *Handbook of Theory and Research for the Sociology of Education*. New York: Greenwood Press.

— (1990), *The Logic of Practice*, trans. R. Nice. Cambridge: Polity Press.

— (1996), *The State Nobility*, trans. L. Clough. Cambridge: Polity Press.

— (1999), *Outline of a Theory of Practice*, trans. R. Nice. Cambridge: Cambridge University Press.

— (2000), *Pascalian Meditations*, trans. R. Nice. Cambridge: Polity Press.

Bourdieu, P. and Passeron, J. (1990), *Reproduction in Education, Society and Culture*, trans. R. Nice. London: Sage.

Bourdieu, P. and Wacquant, L. J. D. (1992), *An Invitation to Reflexive Sociology*. Chicago: University of Chicago Press.

Bowles, S. and Gintis, H. (1976), *Schooling in Capitalist America*. London: Routledge and Kegan Paul.

Brah, A. (1996), *Cartographies of Diaspora*. London: Routledge.

Brannen, J. (2006), Cultures of intergenerational transmission in four-generation families. *The Sociological Review,* 54(1), 133–54.

Brice Heath, S. (1983), *Ways with Words: Language, Life and Work in Communities and Classrooms.* Cambridge: Cambridge University Press.

Brubaker, R. (2004), *Ethnicity without Groups.* Cambridge: Harvard University Press.

Bullivant, B. (1987), *The Ethnic Encounter in the Secondary School.* London: Falmer Press.

— (1988), Ethnic success ethic challenges conventional wisdom about immigrant disadvantage in education. *Australian Journal of Education,* 32(2), 223–43.

Burke, A. (2008), *Fear of Security: Australia's Invasion Anxiety.* Cambridge: Cambridge University Press.

Burrows, L. (2010), 'Kiwi kids are Weet-Bix™ kids' – body matters in childhood. *Sport, Education and Society,* 15(2), 235–51.

Bus, A., van IJzendoorn, M. and Pellegrini, A. (1995), Joint book reading makes for success in learning to read: a meta-analysis on intergenerational transmission of literacy. *Review of Educational Research,* 65(1), 1–21.

Campbell, J. and Verna, M. (2007), Effective parental influence. *Educational Research and Evaluation,* 13(6), 501–19.

Cao, Z., Bishop, A. and Forgasz, H. (2006), Perceived parental influence on mathematics learning: a comparison among students in China and Australia. *Educational Studies in Mathematics,* 64, 85–106.

Cardona, B., Watkins, M. and Noble, G. (2009), *Parents' Perspectives on Schooling.* Centre for Cultural Research, University of Western Sydney, Parramatta.

Charlesworth, Z. (2008), Learning styles across cultures: suggestions for educators. *Education + Training,* 50(2), 115–27.

Choo, O. and Tan, E. (2001), Fathers' role in the school success of adolescents: a Singaporean study. In D. McInerney and S. van Etten (eds), *Research on Sociocultural Influences on Motivation and Learning.* Greenwich: Information Age Publishing, 183–96.

Chua, A. (2011), *Battle Hymn of the Tiger Mother.* London: Bloomsbury.

Clark, R. and Gieve, S. N. (2006) On the discursive construction of 'The Chinese Learner'. *Language, Culture and Curriculum,* 19(1), 54–73.

Coates, R. (2006), Children of immigrant parents and the question of aspirations for the future: understanding segmented assimilation theory from a new perspective. BA Honours thesis, University of Queensland.

Coffield, F., Moseley, D., Hall, E. and Ecclestone, K. (2004), *Learning Styles and Pedagogy in Post-16 learning: A Systematic and Critical Review.* London: Learning and Skills Research Centre.

Collins, J. (2009), Social reproduction in classrooms and schools. *Annual Review of Anthropology,* 38, 33–48.

Collins, J., Noble, G., Poynting, S. and Tabar, P. (2000), *Kebabs, Kids, Cops and Crime.* Annandale, NSW: Pluto Peress.

Collins, S. (2010), Too many Pasifika students falling through cracks, says report. *The New Zealand Herald,* 23 June, p. 2.

Cooper, H. (1989), Synthesis of research of homework. *Educational Leadership,* 47(3), 85–91.

Costigan, C., Hua, J. and Su, T. (2010), Living up to expectations: the strengths and challenges experiences by Chinese Canadian students. *Canadian Journal of School Psychology*, 25, 223–45.

Coxon, E. (2007), Schooling in Samoa. In C. Campbell and G. Sherington (eds), *Going to School in Oceania*. Westport: Greenwood Press, 263–314.

Critcher, C. (2003). *Moral Panics and the Media*. Buckingham: Open University Press.

Cumming, G. (2011). Newest generation shines at top. *The New Zealand Herald*, 12 April, <www.nzherald.co.nz/nz/news/article.cfm?c_id=1&objectid=1071864>.

Cuttance, P. and Stokes, S. (2000), *Reporting on Student and School Achievement*. Canberra: Commonwealth Department of Education, Training and Youth Affairs.

Dandy, J. and Nettelbeck, T. (2002), The relationship between IQ, homework, aspirations and academic achievement for Chinese, Vietnamese and Anglo-Celtic Australian school children. *Educational Psychology*, 22(3), 267–75.

De Graaf, N., De Graaf, P. and Kraaykamp, G. (2000), Parental cultural capital and educational attainment in the Netherlands. *Sociology of Education*, 71, 92–111.

De Lemos, M. (1975), *Study of the Educational Achievement of Migrant Children*. Camberwell, Victoria: ACER.

De Lepervanche, M. (1980), From race to ethnicity in Australian and New Zealand. *Journal of Sociology*, 16(1), 24–37.

Delmas, J. (2003), South Pacific Islander students and science education: addressing the disparity. *NSW Premier's Macquarie Bank Science Scholarship Report*, 89–100.

Department for Education and Skills (DfES) (2006), *Ethnicity and Education: The Evidence on Minority Ethnic Pupils Aged 5–16*. Research Topic Paper, Nottingham.

Dewey, J. (1930), *Human Nature and Conduct: An Introduction to Social Psychology*. New York: The Modern Library.

Disley, J. (2011), Alarm over white pupils pushed to the bottom. *The Daily Express*, 19 January, p. 15.

Doherty, L. (2005), Chinese revolution sweeping our schools. *Sydney Morning Herald*, 26 November, p. 1.

Doherty, C. and Singh, P. (2005), How the West is done: simulating Western pedagogy in a curriculum for Asian international students. In P. Ninnes and M. Hellsten (eds), *Internationalizing Higher Education: Critical Perspectives for Critical Times*. Hong Kong: Hong Kong University Press, 53–74.

Don, T. N., Don, T. and Nishida, T. Y. (1995). *The Asian American Education Experience*. New York: Routledge.

Dooley, K. (2003), Reconceptualising equity: pedagogy for Chinese students in Australian schools. *The Australian Educational Researcher*, 30(3), 25–42.

Dooley, K., Exley, B. and Singh, P. (2000), Social justice and curriculum renewal for Samoan students: an Australian case study. *Special Edition of International Journal of Inclusive Education*, 4(1), 23–42.

Du, L. (2010), *Learning to be Chinese American: Community, Education, and Ethnic Identity*. Lanham: Lexington Books.

Duffy, M. (2001), Improved by Asian work ethic. *Courier Mail*, 29 September, p. 28.

Dumais, S. (2002). Cultural capital, gender, and school success: the role of habitus. *Sociology of Education*, 75(1), 44–68.

Epstein, J., Sanders, M., Sheldon, S. et al. (2009), *School, Family and Community Partnerships: Your Handbook for Action*. Thousand Oaks, CA: Corwin Press.

Evans, J. (2004), Making a difference? Education and 'ability' in physical education. *European Physical Education Review*, 10(1), 95–108.

Fay, G. (2001), Uncovering sociocultural influences leads to a call for personalised learning. In D. McInerney and S. van Etten (eds), *Research on Sociocultural Influences on Motivation and Learning*. Greenwich: Information Age Publishing, 139–58.

Fejgin, N. (1994), Participation in high school competitive sports. *Sociology of Sport Journal*, 11(3), 211–30.

Feng-Bing, S. (2005), *Ethnicity, Children and Habitus: Ethnic Chinese School Children in Northern Ireland*. Bern: Peter Lang.

Ferrari, J. (2007), Parents call for ban on homework. *The Australian*, 10 April, <www.news.com.au/story/0,20876,2152947–421,00.html>

Fisher, A. (2011), Call for Pacific education plan, *Dominion Post*, 21 April, p. 10.

Flockton, L. and Crooks, T. (2001), *Reading and Speaking Assessment Results 2000* (National Education Monitoring Report 19). Wellington, New Zealand: Ministry of Education.

— (2003), *Writing Assessment Results 2002* (National Education Monitoring Report 27). Wellington, New Zealand: Ministry of Education.

Foster, L. and Stockley, D. (1984), *Multiculturalism: The Changing Australian Paradigm*. Clevendon: Multilingual Matters.

Foucault, M. (1977), *Discipline and Punish*, trans. A. Sheridan. Harmondsworth: Penguin Books.

Francis, B. and Archer, L. (2005), British-Chinese pupils' and parents' constructions of the value of education. *British Educational Research Journal*, 31(1), 89–108.

Francis, S. (1995), Pacific Islander young people. In C. Guerra and R. White (eds), *Ethnic Minority Youth in Australia*. Hobart: National Clearinghouse for Youth Studies, 179–92.

Freymark, S. (2011), Are Chinese kids smarter? *Northern District Times*, 2 February, p. 1.

Fynes-Clinton, M. (2011), After the fire, *Courier Mail* Weekend, 9 December, <www.couriermail.com.au/extras/qweekend/fff/features/pdfs/303.pdf>.

Garnaut, J. (2010), China's Confucian culture clash. *The Sydney Morning Herald*, 11–12 December, p. 23.

Garrison, J. W. (2002), Habits as social tools in context. *Occupation, Participation and Health*, 22(4), 11–17.

Gibbs, N. (2011), Roaring tigers, anxious choppers, *Time*, 29 January, <www.time.com/time/magazine/article/0,9171,2043430,00.html>.

Gillies, V. (2005), Raising the 'meritocracy': parenting and the individualization of social class. *Sociology*, 39(5), 835–53.

Gilmore, H. (2009), The China syndrome: the sum of genes, culture, language. *The Sydney Morning Herald*, 24 August, p. 15.

Goldberg, D. (1993), *Racist Culture: Philosophy and the Politics of Meaning*. Oxford: Blackwell.

Goodson, I. and Dowbiggin, I. (1990), Docile bodies: commonalities in the history of psychiatry and schooling. In S. Ball (ed.), *Foucault and Education: Disciplines and Knowledge*. London: Routledge, 105–29.

Gordin, R. D. (1998), Composure: arousal and anxiety dynamic. In M. A. Thompson, R. A. Vernacchia and W. E. Moore (eds), *Case studies in applied sport psychology*. Dubuque, IA: Kendall/Hunt Publishing Company, 37–62.

Gore, J. M. (1998), Disciplining bodies: On the continuity of power relations in pedagogy. In T. S. Pokewitz and M. Brennan (eds), *Foucault's challenge: Discourse, knowledge and power in education*. New York: Teachers College Press, pp. 231–51.

Grant, B. (1997), Disciplining students: the construction of student subjectivities. *British Journal of Sociology of Education*, 18(1), 101–14.

Grenfell, M. and James, D. (1998), Theory, practice and pedagogic research. In M. Grenfell and D. James (eds), *Bourdieu and Education: Acts of Practical Theory*. Bristol: Falmer Press, 6–26.

Grimshaw, T. (2007), Problematizing the construct of 'the Chinese learner': insights from ethnographic research. *Educational Studies*, 33(3), 299–311.

Gutiérrez, K. D. and Rogoff, B. (2003), Cultural ways of learning: individual traits or repertoires of practice. *Educational Researcher*, 32(5), 19–25.

Haines, S. (2011), Confucius say win at all costs. *The Australian*, 19 January, p. 26.

Hall, T. (2009), Real justice is not about custody. *Sydney Morning Herald*, 7 July, p. 11.

Hammer, K. and Friesen, J. (2011), The myth of the brainy immigrant. *The Globe and Mail*, 22 January, <www.theglobeandmail.com/news/national/academic-success-of-east-asian-immigrants-overshadows-struggles-of-others/article1879602>.

Hammond, J. (2001), Scaffolding and language. In J. Hammond (ed.), *Scaffolding*. Newtown, Primary English Teaching Association, 15–30.

Hasan, R. (2009), *Semantic Variation: Meaning in Society and Sociolinguistics*, Vol. 2, in the Collected Works of Ruqaiya Hasan. J. Webster (ed.), London: Equinox.

Haveman, R. and Wolfe, B. (1996). The determinants of children's attainments: a review of methods and findings. *Journal of Economic Literature*, 33(4), 1829–78.

Henderson, A. and Berla, N. (1995), *A New Generation of Evidence: The Family is Critical to Student Achievement*. Washington, DC: National Committee for Citizens in Education.

Hildebrand, J. (2003), Pacific Islanders half of young inmates in western Sydney. *AAP Newsfeed*, 20 June.

Hillier, J. and Rooksby, E. (2005), Introduction. In J. Hillier and E. Rooksby (eds), *Habitus: A Sense of Place*. Aldershot: Ashgate, 19–42.

Hills, L. (2007), Friendship, physicality, and physical education: an exploration of the social and embodied dynamics of girls' physical education experiences. *Sport, Education and Society*, 12(3), 317–36.

Ho, C. (2011), Respecting the presence of others: school micropublics and everyday multiculturalism. *Journal of Intercultural Studies*, 32(6), 603–19.

Holland, A. and Andre, T. (1987). Participation in extra-curricular activities in secondary school. *Review of Educational Research*, 57(4), 437–66.

Holliday, A. R. (2005), *The Struggle to Teach English as an International Language*. Oxford: Oxford University Press.

Holliday, A. R., Hyde, M. and Kullman, J. (2004), *Inter-Cultural Communication: An Advanced Resource Book*. London: Routledge.

Hollinsworth, D. (2006), *Race and Racism in Australia*, 3rd edn. Thomson Social Science Press: South Melbourne.

Hoover-Dempsey, K., Battiato, A., Walker, J., Reed, R., DeJong, J. and Jones, K. (2001), Parental involvement in homework. *Educational Psychologist,* 36, 195–210.

Hoover-Dempsey, K., Walker, J., Sandler, H. and Whetsel, D. (2005), Why do parents become involved? Research findings and implications. *The Elementary School Journal*, 106(2), 105–32.

Hornsby Shire Council (2012), *Community Profile – Epping,* <http://profile. id.com.au/Default.aspx?id=240&pg=103&gid=190&type=enum>.

Horsley, M. and Walker, R. (2004), Pasifika Australia. In D. McInerney and S. van Etten (eds), *Focus on Curriculum*. Greenwich: Information Age Publishing, 327–52.

Houtenville, A. and Conway, K. (2008), Parental effort, school resources, and student achievement. *Journal of Human Resources*, 43(2), 437–53.

Howard, V., McLaughlin, T. and Vacha, E. (1996), Educational capital: a proposed model. *Journal of Behavioral Education,* 6(2), 135–52.

Huntington, S. P. (1997), *The Clash of Civilisations: Remaking the World Order.* New York: Simon and Schuster.

Inglis, C. (2009), Multicultural education in Australia: two generations of evolution. In Banks, J. A. (ed.), *The Routledge International Companion to Multicultural Education*. New York: Routledge, 109–20.

Jackson, S. and Scott, S. (1999), Risk anxiety and the social construction of childhood. In D. Lupton (ed.), *Risk and Sociocultural Theory*. Cambridge: Cambridge University Press.

Jenks, C. (1993), *Culture*. London: Routledge.

Jensen, E. (1988), *Superteaching*. Chatswood: Excellence in Teaching.

Johnson, R., Chambers, D., Raghuram, P. and Tincknell, E. (2004), *The Practice of Cultural Studies*. London: Sage.

Jones, F. (2005), Second-generation immigrant Australians: the socio-economic context, 1986 and 2001. Paper given at the *Second Generation Migrants: Contesting Definitions and Realities* workshop. University of Queensland, Brisbane, 1–2 November.

Kalantzis, M., Cope, B. and Noble, G. (1989), *The Economics of Multicultural Education*. Canberra: Office of Multicultural Affairs, Department of the Prime Minister and Cabinet.

Kalantzis, M., Cope, B., Noble, G. and Poynting, S. (1990), *Cultures of Schooling: Pedagogies for Cultural Difference and Social Access*. London: Falmer Press.

Kalantzis, M. and Cope, B. (1988), Why we need multicultural education. *Journal of Intercultural Studies*, 9(1), 39–57.

Kember, D. (2000), Misconceptions about learning approaches, motivation and study practices of Asian students, *Higher Education*, 40, 99–121.

Khoo, S. and Birrell, B. (2002), The progress of young people of migrant origin in Australia. *People and Place*, 10(2), 32–44.

Kim, S. (2010), Do Asian values exist? Empirical tests of four dimensions of Asian values. *Journal of East Asian Studies,* 10(2), 315–44.

Kluth, P., Straut, D. and Biklen, D. (2003), *Access to Academics for All Students: Critical Approaches to Inclusive Curriculum, Instruction and Policy*. London: Lawrence Erlbaum Associates Publishers.

Ladegaard, H. J. (2012), Discourses of identity: outgroup stereotypes and strategies of discursive boundary-marking in Chinese students' online discussions about 'the other'. *Journal of Multicultural Discourses*, 7(1), 59–79.

Lahire, B. (2010), *The Plural Actor*, trans. D. Fernbach. Cambridge: Polity Press.

Laitsch, D. (2006), Self-discipline and student academic achievement. *Research Brief*, 4(6), <www.ascd.org/>.

Lamb, S., Walstab, A., Teese, R., Vickers, M. and Rumberger, R. (2004), *Staying on at School: Improving Student Retention in Australia*. Report for the Queensland Department of Education and the Arts. Centre for Post-Compulsory Education and Lifelong Learning, The University of Melbourne.

Lane, D. (2006), Islanders in junior leagues, it's a really big issue. *The Sydney Morning Herald*, 16 July, <www.smh.com.au/news/league/islanders-in-junior-leagues-its-a-really-big-issue/2006/07/15/1152637922188.html>.

Lareau, A. (1989), *Home Advantage: Social Class and Parental Intervention in Elementary Education*. New York: Falmer Press.

— (2011), *Unequal Childhoods: Class, race, and Family Life*. Berkeley and Los Angeles, CA: University of California Press.

Lareau, A. and Weininger, E. (2003), Cultural capital in educational research: a critical assessment. *Theory and Society*, 32(5–6), 567–606.

Lau, C. (2011), Confucius say: less homework. *The New Zealand Herald*, 10 May, <www.nzherald.co.nz/college-herald/news/article.cfm?c_id=1502920&objectid=10726661>.

Law, J. (2009), Seeing like a survey. *Cultural Sociology*, 3(2), 239–56.

Lee, J. and Bowen, N. (2006), Parent involvement, cultural capital, and the achievement gap among elementary school children. *American Educational Research Journal*, 43, 193–218.

Lew, J. (2006), Burden of acting neither white nor black: Asian American identities and achievement in urban schools. *The Urban Review*, 38(5), 335–52.

Li, H. (2004), Rethinking silencing silences. In M. Boler (ed.), *Democratic Dialogue in Education: Troubling Speech, Disturbing Silence*. New York: Peter Lang, 69–86.

Louie, V. (2004), *Compelled to Excel: Immigration, Education, and Opportunity among Chinese Americans*. Palo Alto, CA: Stanford University Press.

Lu, L. (2010), Inclusion of a LBOTE related measure in the school SES construct. *Culture, Language and Learning Forum*, NSW Department of Education and Training, 27 October.

Luscombe, B. (2011), Chinese vs Western mothers: Q and A with Amy Chua. *Time*, 11 January.

McClure, J., Meyer, L., Garisch, J., Fischer, R., Weir, K. and Walkey, F. (2011), Students' attributions for their best and worst marks: do they relate to achievement. *Contemporary Educational Psychology*, 36, 71–81.

McInerney, D. and McInerney, V. (1994), *Educational Psychology: Constructing Learning*, Sydney: Prentice-Hall.

McInerney, D. and van Etten, S. (eds) (2001), *Research on Sociocultural Influences on Motivation and Learning*. Greenwich: Information Age Publishing.

McInerney, D., Hinkley, J., Etten, S. and Dowson, M. (1998), Aboriginal, Anglo, and immigrant Australian students' motivational beliefs about personal academic success: are there cultural differences? *Journal of Educational Psychology*, 90(4), 621–9.

McKenzie-Minifie, M. (2007), Pacific Island suspension rate up 20 pc in six years. *The New Zealand Herald*, 1 August, p. 9.

McLeod, J. and Yates, L. (2006), *Making Modern Lives: Subjectivity, Schooling, and Social Change*. Albany: SUNY Press.

McMahon, N. (2011), Mommy dearest? *Sunday Age*, 30 January, p. 13.

McMahon, P. (2011), Chinese voices: Chinese learners and their experiences of living and studying in the United Kingdom. *Journal of Higher Education Policy and Mangagement*, 33(4), 401–14.

Mak, Anson and Mak, Andy (2002), *Filling the Void – The Role of Coaching Centres in the 21st Century*, paper given at Australian Association for Research in Education, Queensland University of Technology, 1–5 December, <www.aare.edu.au/02pap/mak02629.htm>.

Mangina, E. and Mowlds, F. (2007), Sino-Irish teaching dynamics through learning styles awareness. *Multicultural Education & Technology Journal*, 1(4), 222–37.

Marjoribanks, K. (1979), *Ethnic Families and Children's Achievement*. Sydney: Allen and Unwin.

— (2002), *Family and School Capital*. Dordrecht: Springer.

— (2005), Family environments and children's outcomes. *Educational Psychology*, 25(6), 647–57.

Martin, A. (2003), *How to Motivate Your Child for School and Beyond*. Sydney: Bantam Books.

Martin, J. (1978), *The Migrant Presence*. Sydney: George Allen and Unwin.

Martin, J. and Meade, P. (1979), *The Educational Experience of Sydney High School Students*. Canberra: Australian Government Publishing Service.

Matthews, J. (2002), Racialised schooling, 'ethnic success' and Asian–Australian students. *British Journal of Sociology of Education*, 23(2), 193–207.

Mauss, M. (1979), *Sociology and Psychology*, trans. B. Brewster. London: Routledge.

Meo, A. (2011), 'Zafar, so good': middle class students, school habitus and secondary schooling in the city of Buenos. *British Journal of Sociology of Education*, 32(3), 349–67.

Milburn, C. (2010), New arrivals chase a place at the top. *The Age*, 19 July, p. 17.

— (2011), 'Bamboo ceiling' stymies rise to the top. *The Age*, 18 October, p. 15.

Mills, C. (2008) Reproduction and transformation of inequalities in schooling: the transformative potential of the theoretical constructs of Bourdieu. *British Journal of Sociology of Education*, 29(1), 79–89.

Modood, T. (2004), Capitals, ethnic identity and educational qualifications. *Cultural Trends*, 13(2), 87–105.

— (2007), *Multiculturalism, a Civic Idea*. Cambridge: Polity Press.

Morri, M. (2011), Pacific Islanders contribute to Sydney Gang problem, *The Daily Telegraph*, 15 February, <www.dailytelegraph.com.au/news/lawless-sydney-thugs-copy-mayhem-of-us-organised-crime-groups/story-e6freuy9–1226005367695>.

Mortimore, P. (1997), Can effective schools compensate for society? In A. H. Halsey, H. Lauder, P. Brown and A. S. Wells (eds), *Education: Culture, Economy, Society*. Oxford: Oxford University Press.

Munns, G. (2007), A sense of wonder: pedagogies to engage students who live in poverty. *International Journal of Inclusive Education*, 11(3), 301–15.

Murji, K. and Solomos, J. (eds) (2005), *Racialization: Studies in Theory and Practice*. Oxford: Oxford University Press.

Myrberg, E. and Rosen, M. (2009), Direct and indirect effects of parents' education on reading achievement among third graders in Sweden. *British Journal of Educational Psychology*, 79, 695–711.

Nakhid, C. (2003), 'Intercultural' perceptions, academic achievement and the identifying process of Pacific Islands students in New Zealand schools. *Journal of Negro Education*, 72(3), 297–317.

Nash, R. (1999), Bourdieu, 'habitus', and educational research: is it all worth the candle? *British Journal of Sociology of Education*, 20(2), 175–87.

— (2000), Educational inequality: the special case of Pacific students. *Social Policy Journal of New Zealand*, 15, 69–86.

— (2002a), The educated habitus, progress at school, and real knowledge. *Interchange*, 33(1), 27–48.

— (2002b), Disposed to succeed: a realist discourse on progress at school. *Change: Transformations in Education*, 5(2), 25–38.

Nasir, N. S. and Saxe, G. B. (2003), Ethnic and academic identities: a cultural practice perspective on emerging tensions and their management in the lives of minority students. *Educational Researcher*, 32(5), 14–18.

Neill, R. (2011), Incessant is the mother of invective, *The Australian*, 12 February, <www.theaustralian.com.au/arts/books/incessant-is-the-mother-of-invective/story-e6frg8nf-1226001570142>.

New South Wales Department of School Education Metropolitan West Region (1992), *Accelerative Learning Initiative Level 1 Training*. Sydney: Mount Druitt Educational Resource Centre.

Nichols, L. (2006), Another brick in the wall; they say cultural identity ignored. *Dominion Post*, 9 December, p. 8.

Nichols, L. and Bennetts, J. (2006) Polynesians lag behind at school. *The Press*, 6 December, p. 6.

Noble, G. (2011), 'Bumping into Alterity': transacting cultural complexities. *Continuum*, 25(6), 827–40.

Noble, G. and Poynting, S. (2000), Multicultural eduction and intercultural understanding: ethnicity, culture and schooling. In S. Dinham and C. Scott (eds), *Teaching in Context*. Camberwell, Victoria: ACER Press, 56–81.

Noble, G. and Watkins, M. (2003), So, how did Bourdieu learn to play tennis? Habitus, consciousness and habituation, *Cultural Studies*, 17(3/4), 520–38.

— (2013), The 'schooled identities' of Australian multiculturalism: professional vision, reflexive civility and education for a culturally complex world. In V. Lander and R. Race (eds), *Advancing Race, Ethnicity and Education*. Houndmills: Palgrave Macmillan.

North, S. and Pillay, H. (2002), Homework: re-examining the routine. *ELT Journal*, 56(2), 137–45.

Northern District Times (2002), Ethnic bias in change. *Northern District Times*, 21 August, p. 8.

— (2012), Poll archive, <http://northern-district-times.whereilive.com.au/polls/>.

O'Farrell, C., Meadmore, D., McWilliam, E. and Symes, C. (eds) (2000), *Taught Bodies*. New York: Peter Lang.

Ofahengaue Vakalahi, H. F. (2009), Pacific Islander American students: caught between a rock and a hard place? *Children and Youth Services Review*, 31, 1258–63.

Oldham, J. (2011) 'Tiger Mother' meets reality: Asian students struggle, too. *McClatchy*. Washington Bureau, <www.mcclatchydc.com/2011/02/11/v-print/108556/tiger-mother-meets-reality-asian.html>.

O'Neill, S. (2009), Pacifika program endeavours to keep kids out of jail, *7.30 Report, ABC*, 7 July.

Ong, A. (2006), *Neoliberalism as Exception: Mutations in Citizenship and Sovereignty*. Durham: Duke University Press.

Organisation for Economic Co-operation and Development (2006), *Where Immigrant Students Succeed – A Comparative Review of Performance and Engagement in PISA, 2003*. Paris: OECD Publications.

Pang, V. O., Han, P. P. and Pang, J. M. (2011), Asian American and Pacific Islander students: equity and the achievement gap. *Educational Researcher*, 40(8), 378–89.

Parekh, B. (2002), *Rethinking Multiculturalism: Cultural Diversity and Political Theory*. Basingstoke: Macmillan.

Parramatta City Council (2012), *Community Profile – Epping*, <http://profile.id.com.au/Default.aspx?id=265&pg=103&gid=150&type=enum>.

Partington, G. and McCudden, V. (1992), *Ethnicity and Education*. Wentworth Falls, NSW: Social Science Press.

Patty, A. (2008a), Parent who bribed teacher buckled under peer pressure: selective schools. *The Sydney Morning Herald*, 13 December, p. 9.

— (2008b), White flight from schools. *The Sydney Morning Herald*, 10 March, p. 1.

— (2009), Parents make moves on top schools: back to class. *The Sydney Morning Herald*, 28 January, p. 3.

Paul, A. (2011), Tiger moms: is tough parenting really the answer? *Time*, 20 January.

Powell, B. (2011), An American dad on raising a Tiger daughter. *Time*, 20 January.

Poynting, S. and Noble, G. (1998), 'Rekindling the spark': teachers' experiences of accelerative learning. *Australian Journal of Education*, 42(1), 32–48.

Preston, N. and Symes, C. (1994), *Schools and Classroom*. Melbourne: Longman Cheshire.

Prout, A. (2000) (ed.), *The Body, Childhood and Society*. London: Macmillan.

Reay, D. (1995), They employ cleaners to do that: habitus in the primary classroom. *British Journal of Sociology of Education*, 16, 353–71.

— (1998), Cultural reproduction. In M. Grenfell and D. James (eds), *Bourdieu and Education: Acts of Practical Theory*. Bristol: Falmer Press, 55–71.

— (2004), Education and cultural capital. *Cultural Trends*, 13(2), 73–86.

Reed, T. (2011), Achievement gap persists. *The Capital* (Annapolis), 15 September, <http://global.factiva.com/aa/?ref=CPGN000020110915e79f0003c&pp=1&fcpil=en&napc=S&sa_from=>.

Reed-Danahay, D. (2005). *Locating Bourdieu*. Bloomington, IN: Indiana University Press.

Reschly, A. L. and Christenson, S. L. (2009), Parents as essential partners for fostering students' learning outcomes. In M. Furlong, R. Gilman and E. S. Huebner (eds), *A Handbook of Positive Psychology in Schools*. New York: Routledge, 257–72.

Robinson, K. (2000), Looking for father-right: the Asian values debate and Australia–Asia Relations. In J. Docker and G. Ischer (eds), *Race, Colour and Identity in Australia and New Zealand*. Kensington: University of New South Wales Press, 158–73.

— (2010), Pacific Islander elders in bid to stop crime on streets. *Manly Daily*, 19 November, <http://manly-daily.whereilive.com.au/news/story/pacific-islander-elders-in-bid-to-stop-crime-on-streets/>.

Rosenthal, D. and Feldman, S. (1991), The influence of perceived family and personal factors on self-reported school performance of Chinese and Western high school students. *Journal of Research on Adolescence*, 1(2), 135–54.

Rowlands, L. (2011), Parenting is more than punishing to perfection. *Daily Telegraph*, 1 January, p. 29.

Salili, F. (1996), Accepting personal responsibility for learning. In D. A. Watkins and J. B. Biggs (eds), *The Chinese Learner: Cultural Psychological and Contextual Influences*. Melbourne: ACER, 85–106.

Schellenberg, E. G. (2004), Music lessons enhance IQ. *Psychological Science*, 15(8), 511–14.

Scherger, S. and Savage, M. (2010), Cultural transmission, educational attainment and social mobility. *The Sociological Review*, 58(3), 406–28.

Schneider, B. and Lee, Y. (1990), A model for academic success: the school and home environment of East Asian students. *Anthropology and Education Quarterly*, 21(4), 358–77.

Seamon, D. (2002), Physical comminglings: body, habit, and space transferred into place. *OTJR: Occupation, Participation and Health*, 22(4), 42–51.

Shah, B., Dwyer, C. and Modood, T. (2010), Explaining educational achievement and career aspirations among young British Pakistanis: mobilizing 'ethnic capital'? *Sociology*, 44, 1109–27.

Sheldon, S. and Epstein, J. (2005), Involvement counts: family and community partnerships and mathematic achievement. *The Journal of Educational Research*, 98(4), 196–207.

Shilling, C. (2004), Physical capital and situated action: a new direction for corporeal sociology. *British Journal of Sociology of Education*, 25(3), 473–87.

Sibley, B. A. and Etnier, J. L. (2003), The relationship between physical activity and cognition in children: a meta-analysis. *Pediatric Exercise Science*, 15, 243–56.

Simon, P. and Piché, V. (2012), Accounting for ethnic and racial diversity: the challenge of enumeration. *Ethnic and Racial Studies*, 35(8), 1357–65.

Singh, P. (2001), Speaking about cultural difference and school disadvantage. An interview study of 'Samoan' paraprofessionals in designated disadvantaged secondary schools in Australia. *British Journal of Sociology of Education*, 22(3), 317–37.

Singh, P. and Sinclair, M. (2001), Diversity, disadvantage and differential outcomes. *Asia-Pacific Journal of Teacher Education*, 29(1), 73–92.

Solomos, J. and Back, L. (1996), *Racism and society*. Houndmills: Palgrave Macmillan.

Stevenson, A. and Patty, A. (2010), The chosen ones, *The Sydney Morning Herald*, 3 July, p. 11.

Sticht, T. G. (1988), Adult literacy education. *Review of Research in Education*, 15, 59–96.

Strand, S. (2007), Minority ethnic pupils in the longitudinal study of young people in England. *Report for the Department for Children, Schools and Families*, University of Warwick.

Strom, H. (2001), Perceived parenting success of mothers in Japan. In D. McInerney and S. van Etten (eds), *Research on Sociocultural Influences on Motivation and Learning*. Greenwich: Information Age Publishing, 161–82.

Sue, S. and Okazaki, S. (1990), Asian-American educational achievement. *American Psychologist*, 45(8), 913–20.

Sun, J. (2011), Studying is the key. *Northern District Times*, 2 February, p. 2.

Tamayo-Lott, J. (1998), *Asian Americans: From Racial Category to Multiple Identities*. New York: Altamira Press.

Taras, H. (2005), Physical activity and student performance at school. *The Journal of School Health*, 75(6), 214–18.

Teese, R. (2007), Time and space in the reproduction of educational inequality. In M. Duru-Bellat, S. Lamb and R. Teese (eds), *International Studies in Educational Inequality, Theory and Policy. Vol. 1: Educational Inequality: Persistence and Change*. Dordrecht: Springer, 1–23.

Thrupp, M. (1998), The art of the possible: organising and managing high and low socio-economic schools. *Journal of Education Policy*, 13(2), 197–219.

Tiwari, A., Avery, A. and Lai, P. (2003), Critical thinking disposition of Hong Kong Chinese and Australian nursing students. *Journal of Advanced Nursing*, 44(3), 298–307.

Tomkins, S. (1962), *Affect, Imagery and Consciousness. Vol. 1: The Positive Affects*. New York: Springer Publishing Company.

Trudeau, F. and Shephard, R. (2008), Physical education, school physical activity, school sports and academic performance. *International Journal of Behavioral Nutrition and Physical Activity*, 5(1), 10–19.

Urdan, T. and Giancarlo, C. (2001), A comparison of motivational and critical thinking orientations across ethnic groups. In D. McInerney and S. van Etten (eds), *Research on Sociocultural Influences on Motivation and Learning*. Greenwich: Information Age Publishing, 37–60.

Valdez, M., Dowrick, P. and Maynard, A. (2007), Cultural misperceptions and goals for Samoan children's education in Hawaii: voices from school, home, and community. *The Urban Review*, 39(1), 67–92.

Wall, E., Ferrazzi, G. and Schryer, F. (1998), Getting the goods on social capital. *Rural Sociology*, 63(2), 300–22.

Wallace, I. (2008), Asian values get results. *The Courier Mail*, 18 January, <www.news.com.au/couriermail/story/0,23739,23067479-27197,00.html>.

Watkins, D. A. and Biggs, J. B. (2001), The paradox of the Chinese learner and beyond. In D. A. Watkins and J. B. Biggs (eds), *Teaching the Chinese Learner: Psychological and Pedagogical Perspectives*. Camberwell, Melbourne: ACER, 3–23.

Watkins, D. A., Regmi, M. and Astilla, E. (1991), The Asian-learner-as-a-rote-learner stereotype: myth or reality? *Educational Psychology*, 11, 21–34.

Watkins, M. (2005a), Discipline, consciousness and the formation of a scholarly habitus. *Continuum*, 19(4), 545–58.

— (2005b), The erasure of habit: tracing the pedagogic body. *Discourse: Studies in the Cultural Politics of Education*, 26(2), 167–81.

— (2010), Discipline, diversity and agency: pedagogic practice and dispositions to learning. In Z. Millei, T. G. Griffiths, and R. J. Parkes (eds), *Re-Theorising Discipline in Education: Problems, Politics and Possibilities*. New York: Peter Lang, 59–75.

— (2011a), Complexity reduction, regularities and rules: trying to make sense of cultural diversity in schooling. *Continuum: Journal of Media and Cultural Studies*, 25(6), 841–56.

— (2011b), *Discipline and Learn: Bodies, Pedagogy and Writing*. Rotterdam: Sense Publications.

Watkins, M. and Noble, G. (2011a), The productivity of stillness: composure and the scholarly habitus. In D. Bissell and G. Fuller (eds), *Stillness in a Mobile World*. London: Routledge, 107–24.

— (2011b), Losing touch: pedagogies of incorporation and the ability to write. *Social Semiotics*, 21(4), 503–16.

White, R., Perrone, S., Guerra, C., Francis, S., Hunter, F. and Lampugnani, R. (1999), Ethnic youth Gangs in Australia – do they exist? *Report No. 3: Pacific Islander Young People*. Melbourne: Australian Multicultural Foundation.

Wicker, R. (1997), From complex culture to cultural complexity. In P. Werbner and T. Modood (eds), *Debating Cultural Hybridity: Multicultural Identities and the Politics of Anti-Racism*. London: Zed Books, 29–45.

Windle, J. (2004), The ethnic (dis)advantage debate revisited: Turkish background students in Australia. *Journal of Intercultural Studies,* 25(3), 271–86.

— (2008), The management and legitimisation of educational inequalities in Australia: some implications for school experience. *International Studies in Sociology of Education*, 18(3–4), 157–71.

Wing On, L. (1996), The cultural context for Chinese learners: conceptions of learning in the Confucian tradition. In D. A. Watkins and J. B. Biggs (eds), *The Chinese Learner: Cultural Psychological and Contextual Influences*. Melbourne: ACER, 25–41.

Woodrow, D. and Sham, S. (2001), Chinese pupils and their learning preferences. *Race Ethnicity and Education,* 4(4), 377–94.

Wright, J. E. (2004), Poststructuralist methodologies: the body, schooling and health. In J. Evans, B. Davies and J. E. Wright (eds), *Body Knowledge and Control: Studies in the Sociology of Physical Education and Health*. London: Routledge, 19–32.

Wu, J. and Singh, M. (2004), 'Wishing for Dragon Children': ironies and contradictions in China's educational reforms and the Chinese diaspora's disappointments with Australian education. *The Australian Educational Researcher*, 31(2), 29–44.

Xu, J. and Corno, L. (1998), Case studies of families doing third-grade homework. *Teachers College Record*, 100(2), 402–36.

— (2003), Family help and homework management reported by middle school students. *The Elementary School Journal*, 103(5), 503–17.

Yaman, E. (2002), Selected for their strengths – the cultural divide. *The Australian*, 10 May, p. 10.

Yu, T. (2006), Challenging the politics of the 'Model Minority' stereotype: a case for educational equality. *Equity and Excellence in Education*, 39, 325–33.

Zhao, D. and Singh, M. (2011), Why do Chinese-Australian students outperform their Australian peers in mathematics: a comparative case study. *International Journal of Science and Mathematics Education*, 9(1), 69–87.

Zhao, D., Mulligan, J. and Mitchelmore, M. (2006), Case studies on mathematics assessment practices in Australian and Chinese primary schools. In F. Leung, K. Graf and F. Lopez-Real (eds), *Mathematics Education in Different Cultural Traditions*. Netherlands: Springer, 261–75.

Index

aspirations and 62–7
parental engagement with school
  and 47–8
parents backgrounds and 40–2
survey 39–40
educational outcomes 67–9
embodied dispositions, to
  learning 136–8
engagement
  and control 130–1
  definition of 128
  discipline of 121–3
  in learning 126–8
English as Second Language
  (ESL) 15, 123, 126, 130
English-speaking background (ESB) 2,
  5, 16, 26, 68
Epstein, J. 39
ethnicity *see individual entries*
Etnier, J. L. 45
Evans, J. 7, 53

Fay, G. 38
Fejgin, N. 45
Feldman, S. 3, 36, 62
Feng-Bing, S. 70
Ferrari, J. 72
Fisher, A. 4, 28, 29
Flockton, L. 3, 36
Foster, L. 16
Foucault, M. 8, 80, 117, 139
Francis, B. 3, 35, 36, 96, 109
Francis, S. 4
Freymark, S. 19
Friesen, J. 16, 21
Fynes-Clinton, M. 27

Garnaut, J. 25
Garrison, J. W. 79
Giancarlo, C. 51
Gibbs, N. 18
Gieve, S. N. 20, 25
Gillies, V. 78
Gilmore, H. 26
Gintis, H. 38, 41, 42
Globe 21
Goldberg, D. 4
Goodson, I. 7
Gordin, R. D. 57
Gore, J. M. 8

Grant, B. 141
Grenfell, M. 52
Grimshaw, T. 3, 99
Gutiérrez, K. D. 2, 100, 101

habitus 6–14, 38, 43, 52–4, 57, 59, 60,
  62, 69–72, 75, 78–82, 90–1, 97,
  113, 114, 116–19, 129, 131, 135,
  141–2, 143n. 2, 144n. 2 (Chapter 3)
  see also scholarly habitus
Haines, S. 25
Hall 4
Hammer, K. 16, 21
Hammond, J. 96, 120
Hasan, R. 145n. 1
Haveman, R. 41
Hawke, B. 24
Henderson, A. 39
Hildebrand, J. 4, 27
Hill, B. 15
Hillier, J. 62
Hills, L. 53
Ho, C. 26
Hodkinson, P. 7, 52, 131
Holland, A. 45
Holliday, A. R. 31, 133
Hollinsworth, D. 4
home
  and cultural capital 38
  and homework, habits of 72–7
Hoover-Dempsey, K. 43, 77, 83
Hornsby Shire Council 144n. 2
  (Chapter 1)
Horsley, M. 3, 36
Houtenville, A. 44
Howard, V. 38
Huntington, S. P. 17

Inglis, C. 15

Jackson, S. 22
James, D. 52
Jenks, C. 5
Jensen, E. 2
Johnson, R. 12
Jones, F. 35, 54

Kalantzis, M. 2, 35, 47, 53
Kawakami, A. J. 78
Kember, D. 99